&Personal
&Social
Education

Acknowledgements

I am indebted to: Peter Mann, Principal Adviser of Dorset LEA and to Bill Copland, Senior Adviser for Secondary Schools in Dorset, for their painstaking comments on the manuscript; Jack Whitehead of the University of Bath for his endless encouragement and good humour; Robert Royce for his continual support in the preparation of the manuscript.

I would like to thank Rodney Cocks, Adviser for Religious, Personal and Social Education in Dorset, who contributed much to my thinking about models for personal and social education in schools.

Many of the thoughts I have expressed in part 2B (Basic principles and management skills) began in 1970 when I worked with Robert O'Neill who developed the idea of 'teaching goal' in the Eurocentre's R & D team.

Most of all I thank the teachers with whom I have been privileged to work. I have learnt much, and still have much to learn.

CRAC publications are published under exclusive licence and royalty agreements by Hobsons Limited. The Careers Research and Advisory Centre is an independent non-profit-making body.

First published in 1985 by Hobsons Limited Bateman Street Cambridge CB2 1LZ

ISBN 0 86021 820 1
Ref: N435/n·15c/A/HF

Sometimes the masculine pronoun is used in the text where the reference might more accurately refer to both sexes. This is to avoid tortuous, repetitive sentence structure peppered with 'he or she'. Unless otherwise specified readers should construe the reference 'he' as applying equally to both sexes.

&Personal Social Education

— A teacher's handbook
Jean McNiff

CRAC

Hobsons Cambridge

■■■■■■■■■Contents■■■■■■■■■

Part 2 Good Practice

Contents

Contents

Introduction

Personal and social education is a priority area in current educational thinking. It is at the heart of the curriculum as an aspect that may contribute significantly to the well-being of children in schools. Documents produced by national and government bodies recommend that personal and social education should enjoy a central place on the curriculum, and these recommendations are reflected more and more frequently in the policy statements of Local Education Authorities and of individual schools.

The emphasis seems to be changing in educational aims and objectives. The curriculum still encourages academic excellence, but aims also to develop a personal competence in young people, an ability to respond to the world with honesty, spontaneity and pleasure. The difficulty for class teachers arises in translating the theory of these aims into the practice of their classrooms. Recommendations, aims and objectives are frequently couched in abstract terms. What does 'personal development' mean, for example? How do we recognise it? More difficult still, how do we teach for it? The literature tells us what we might expect as 'end behaviour', but there is little guidance as to how we may help to bring it about.

Schools often find themselves in confusion over personal and social education; whether it is a 'subject' with a specific content and a set of attitudes, or a random body of skills and knowledge that are acquired through other areas of the curriculum. There is controversy over who should teach it, whether teachers should be tutors, whether it will do anything towards enhancing the quality of the children's lives. Without doubt, personal and social education is potentially one of the most powerful vehicles for change in our current educational thinking, and, with encouragement, teachers can be mighty agents for change in society.

This book is an attempt to bridge the gap between the theory and the practice of personal and social education. It looks at some theoretical considerations and attempts to provide some answers on translating that theory into the reality of the classroom. True to its message that our job as teachers is not so much to teach our children what to think as how to think, the book does not take any particular stand on the issues; rather it attempts to clarify the options for teachers themselves to decide on which course of action to follow.

In brief, if a school is considering introducing personal and social education onto its curriculum, either formally or informally, the book airs a number of issues, and suggests practical ways of answering many questions that will arise.

PART 1

Considerations

A

Personal and social education in secondary schools: some important issues

The academic curriculum and the hidden curriculum

Most schools organise their curricula at two levels: the academic curriculum and the hidden curriculum. Most of us know what is expected of us in an academic curriculum. There is usually a written syllabus and a clear structure to the departmental organisation. We have been given training in the subject area, and we receive further training from more experienced members of staff as we go along through the school. Perhaps we come to grief at times, but in terms of content and organisation, the subject matter is previously specified and implementable.

The same cannot be said for many of us in positions of pastoral responsibility, or involved in teaching personal and social education. Aspects of pastoral education lie within the hidden curriculum, and it is not always easy for teachers to see clearly what is expected of them.

This lack of clearly defined aims seems to be a reason for the tentative approach to personal and social education in schools; most are not nearly so confident about the content and organisation of pastoral areas as they are about the academic subjects they offer. There is no common syllabus for personal and social education, no commonly-agreed criteria to say that personal development has been achieved, no examination.

Recently I undertook an evaluation of a local school's scheme of personal and social education. I arranged a staff meeting to discuss what procedures we were going to adopt, and what we were going to evaluate. That meeting brought home to us all just how difficult the exercise was.

Our procedure was quite straightforward: we would eventually involve all members of staff, but in the first instance we would focus only on a team of one year-group of teachers. That made the exercise manageable. These teachers would look at their aims in personal and social education, analyse what they were doing in their class practice, and see how closely these two elements matched.

This is where we ran into some considerable difficulty.

It had been easy, as an academic exercise, to draw up a list of aims. We all agreed, for example, that:
1 children should enjoy the experience of school;
2 children should develop to the limit of their potential;
3 the school should accept the responsibility for the welfare of each and every child.

Altogether there were about 25 items in the list.

There was no doubt that all teachers agreed that they were aiming to implement the statements in their class practice. Where they disagreed was in their understanding of the aims, and in what they were doing in order to achieve them. There was no consensus as to what 'the limit of their potential' meant, for example, nor of the implications of statement 3: who should accept the responsibility, what did 'welfare' mean, and to what extent was the school to be responsible? The confusion increased when we looked specifically at how we hoped to realise these aims. What exactly did we do in lessons to help children develop to the limit of their potential, and how would we recognise it when they did? Our evaluation caused a lot of healthy discussion. Before we began judging whether our class practice lived up to our aims, we had to be more pragmatic in our analysis of those aims. We had to be quite specific about what we all agreed by 'personal development'.

This school, as a result, developed a two-tier system of aims; they kept the rather abstract notions of 'personal development' and 'full potential' and 'enjoyment of school experience' as the overall aims of the education they offered. They were much more specific about the aims of their scheme of personal and social education, expressing it in working definitions of skills, attitudes and competencies. For example, they suggested certain *behaviours* as outcomes of their scheme; that the children should listen to each other; that they should be literate and numerate to a specified degree; that they should show responsible attitudes in class; and so on.

What was evident through this school's experience was a paradox that faces many schools: they are aware that personal and social education is fundamental to a child's personal, academic and social development, yet it is probably the most difficult aspect of the school curriculum to define or assess.

Following on from this, let us begin by looking at some aims and objectives.

The aims of education

A number of national and regional documents give us clear indications as to what are seen as fundamental aims of education. Some of these documents are listed in the Bibliography, section 1.3; two here suffice as examples:

The Warnock Report This report was written with respect to children with special needs, but this comment is relevant to the educational needs of all children:

> First, to enlarge a child's knowledge, experience and imaginative understanding and then his awareness of moral values and capacity for enjoyment; secondly, to enable him to enter the world after formal education is over as an active participant in society and a responsible contributor to it, capable of achieving as much independence as possible.

A framework for the curriculum This report is a recent government statement on schools' curricula, and contains the following guidelines for the aims of education:

1 to help pupils to develop lively, inquiring minds, the ability to question and argue rationally and to apply themselves to tasks and physical skills;
2 to help pupils acquire knowledge and skills relevant to adult life and employment in a fast-changing world;
3 to help pupils to use language and number effectively;
4 to instil respect for religious and moral values, and tolerance of other races, religions and ways of life;
5 to help pupils understand the world in which they live, and the interdependence of individuals, groups and nations;
6 to help pupils appreciate human achievements and aspirations.

These recommendations are reflected in the curriculum policy statements of many Local Education Authorities.

The aims of personal and social education

The aims of personal and social education are not so concretely formulated as the aims of education; but it is clear on reading published recommendations about personal and social education in documents about the general aims of education, that those recommendations reflect the values inherent in the broad aims of education. Personal and social education attempts to show those aims in practice.

For example:

Curriculum 11–16 comments on the 'socialisation of the young, their induction into adulthood, and their preparation as citizens, parents, wage earners, and voters of the future'.

A View of the Curriculum says that 'schools need to secure for all pupils opportunities for learning particularly likely to contribute to personal and social development'.

Aspects of Secondary Education in England states that 'teachers generally acknowledge . . . the need to provide more personal education in the curriculum of all pupils'.

Local Education Authorities incorporate these recommendations into their own policy statements and publish them in terms of aims. Dorset provides comprehensive guidance, of which the following is a part:

> Personal education . . . should aim to foster the . . . process by which a child, through experience, builds his own awareness and realisation of himself as a more or less autonomous individual.

Translating aims into action

There is a problem, however, in that personal and social education has a wide-ranging definition. How should schools translate those recommendations into action? For example, where in the day do we teach for self-realisation or confidence or sensitivity, or any of the other qualities that are implied in those published recommendations? Do we teach them in sessions of personal and social education, or in English, or in mathematics, or is it an informal process taught by example?

In the evaluation mentioned earlier, a colleague, a teacher of English and drama, commented: 'I know what I am doing in English. I have a syllabus to get through and I know how to teach to that syllabus. I know what I am doing in drama. I do there a lot of the things we have looked at in our pastoral workshops. Yet I don't know what is expected of me in tutorial time. I constantly switch from confusion and vagueness about social education to a certainty that I am already overlapping in my English and drama.' This is an observation often made by teachers (see page 33) and it highlights the need for schools to develop a coherent pastoral system. In deciding to implement any pastoral scheme such as personal and social education, schools must look at what they are doing throughout the whole of school life so that their effect on the children is as positive and beneficial as possible.

A coherent pastoral system

Increasingly, schools are aware of the need to provide a coherent, monitorable approach to the whole pastoral system in secondary schools. This would include the organisation of pastoral tutors, the organisation of the teaching of specific content such as health education, and the organisation of the teaching of attitudes and values. In academic subjects, all self-respecting heads of department plan their syllabuses carefully, constantly reviewing and evaluating progress. It follows that a similar process ought to be in operation for the pastoral aspects within the total school framework. Indeed, this would seem to be more necessary with the ever-increasing burden of responsibility on schools for the social, moral and emotional development and well-being of their pupils. Pupils, too, need to be aware of whom they can go to for help, and teachers need to know where they stand. Pastoral care for teachers is important, too.

A co-ordinated approach is essential, but that approach must always be left up to individual schools to decide on. One school might adopt a year base for its pastoral organisation, while another might choose a house system. One might have a credit system for rewards and motivation; others might have a record of personal development. No two schools are sufficiently alike for detailed common policies to be applicable, and they are wise to adapt existing schemes such as appear in the literature to their own needs. Certainly schools would share common aims and values, and would agree to common aspects of good practice; but there must always be the flexibility to allow schools and individual teachers to adapt guidelines arising from these shared practices according to their own needs.

This would be true, also, of a school policy of personal and social education: within a commonly agreed framework, an individual teacher, or group of teachers, would have the freedom of flexibility to select or reject out of any scheme that which they felt appropriate or not to the needs of their pupils. No scheme should ever be so rigidly inflexible as to dictate what is to be taught when and by whom. Spontaneity and sincerity must be fundamental to all class practice, and to sacrifice the needs of the children to the rigours of the scheme would be to deny the very aims of the education we are seeking to give.

What, then, of the problem outlined above that schools will have different views of the function within the curriculum of personal and social education? I take the view that academic subjects should be taught against the backdrop of care and support that are the cornerstones of personal and social education; that, ideally, personal and social education should be taught through the whole curriculum, and not as an isolated subject. Ideally, schools should share the fundamental ethos that education is about the love, care and support of each and every child; instruction must come second to welfare. Academic instruction might thus be seen as a part of this framework of care, and personal and social education as an inherent value-system for the whole school.

With this view of the position of personal and social education in schools in mind, we should now consider two aspects of its implementation: short-term means to long-term ends, and the curriculum content.

Short-term means to long-term ends

Pastoral care may be viewed as the whole caring atmosphere between teachers and pupils, and pupils and pupils, covering all the inter-relationships operating in a school. Personal and social education may be viewed as a specific input, whichever slot it may occupy on the timetable, where pupils practise the skills and attitudes that go towards creating and maintaining this overall caring atmosphere.

Ideally, perhaps, personal and social education ought not to be necessary as a specific input, since the values of care and support should be so firmly a part of the school's underlying ethos that time-tabled sessions should be unnecessary. The school would already be realising its basic aims in its everyday life, easily translating theoretical aims into real practice. Unfortunately this is not always the case.

A sensible approach would be for schools to look for short-term means to long-term ends. If personal and social education is a medium to get across the values of the school's curriculum, then a short-term input of personal and social education 'lessons' would be a strategy to achieve the long-term aims of fundamental care and support.

The process of personal and social education

A basic characteristic of personal and social education is that it is a *process* rather than a *content*. Traditionally, the school curriculum has been arranged in terms of content. Today the curriculum is widening its focus to put more emphasis on skills, concepts and attitudes. This can be seen in our 16-plus examination criteria, and personal and social education reflects this view.

The learning experience itself is the content of personal and social education. In order to understand the content the pupils have to go through the process itself. They cannot learn about relationships unless they experience relationships; they will not appreciate concepts such as 'kindness' or 'empathy' unless they experience those emotions. The starting point for any scheme of personal and social education, whether that scheme is relatively simple, such as a programme of basic hygiene, or very sophisticated, as in a social skills training programme, is to engage the young people's attention and commitment. This personal involvement in what is learnt is crucial to success.

It is of great importance that this is recognised. For example, in a discussion, the most important feature is that children talk to each other; that they are at liberty to talk about things within the supportive framework of the group, without fear of ridicule or emotional destruction. A much less important aspect of talking time among the pupils is that they should reach a consensus. Traditionally, perhaps, an agreed opinion at the end of the day is seen as the prime objective. Personal and social education works towards activating children's minds, developing their listening skills, helping them to be sensitive to each other and tolerant. The least important aspect in discussion sessions is probably the teacher's voice. Similarly, in all such schemes, emphasis should necessarily be on pupils' involvement in the learning process, rather than on the content of the programme.

Nevertheless, schools look for guidance in deciding what should be done in their schemes of personal and social education. On in-service courses that I am involved in, one of the most welcomed features is an explanation of other people's schemes. Colleagues compare their own practice against that of other schools. Teachers often worry whether it is legitimate to incorporate certain aspects into their schemes. Is it all right to include health education or safety or preparation for Christmas? Or do those aspects not qualify? Schools need reassurance that they are doing the right thing in deciding what goes into their overall schemes.

For this we could follow through a few simple questions:

1 *If we did not exist as pastoral tutors and supervisors, would our pupils still manage without us?*

   The answer to this question is certainly yes. Pupils will get by without us, and cope very well.

2 *If they can get by, then can we identify those areas where our involvement in their lives will enhance the quality of their experience?*

   To answer this we need to ask ourselves if we can be more valuable than parents, friends, mass media, and in which particular situation. When do the children need us most?

3 *Having identified the areas of the children's need on an individual as well as a group basis, then how can we best accelerate the learning process?*

This aspect of acceleration is very important. What is needed is for the school to decide on those areas where children most need us, as in questions 1 and 2, and then concentrate there. It is wasteful of resources to focus on minor aspects.

This is where it is so important for schools to define their own criteria as to what is most or least important to them. For example, School A may feel that personal politeness is crucial to children's development; School B may accept that it is desirable but not of central importance. School C may decide that study skills are essential in year 1; School D may not see the need for close attention to study skills until year 3. Some schools would regard their schemes of personal and social education as running throughout the child's school life. Other schools would regard personal and social education as only the establishment and maintenance of relationships. Yet others would focus on the knowledge aspects of how to get on, for example, in form filling and letter writing. Once the individual school's priorities have been identified, then personal and social education accelerates the acquisition of skills in dealing with these aspects.

The function of personal and social education

The *function* of personal and social education might be defined in at least two ways: in terms of crisis prevention, and in terms of social competence.

The first aspect would focus on the establishment of relationships, on encouraging attitudes appropriate to the well-being of society, on training pupils to cope with stressful situations and how to avoid them. The second aspect would focus on the development of specific social competencies to empower the pupils to realise their full potential in a complex and fast-changing society. Clearly, the two aspects overlap at many points, since avoidance of crises may highlight specific behaviours which themselves may be termed 'coping strategies'; the pupils will be encouraged to develop their repertoire of social skills in finding out how to avoid possible social conflict. For example, a class may be looking at a possible conflict arising between parent and child if the child comes home later than the agreed time. The activity here may be to examine the reasons why parents request children to be home at a certain time, and to highlight elements of consideration and smooth family management. At the same time, the skill of avoiding rows and the encouragement of tactful exchanges may be developed. Through practice in avoidance of crises, pupils may also discover new modes of behaviour which will enrich their experience and understanding of others' points of view.

Practice in crisis avoidance is often viewed as an answer to some of the social ills that attack schools and the children in them. Many teachers share hopes that the children they teach should be sensitive and tolerant to the needs of each other; that they should genuinely enjoy their school experience; that they should share alert and positive attitudes, working for their own self-realisation and for the common good. Unfortunately, in practice, teachers are confronted daily by a denial of their educational values in the attitudes of many of their pupils. These attitudes are further encouraged by the public voices of politicians, advertisers and trend-setters, who attack youngsters through the media and are often counterproductive to the values of care that teachers are trying to encourage in schools.

Looking at the social life in schools, then, there is often a clear need for specific input of care and support, and this can happen through a session of personal and social education. Colleagues have remarked, 'We realise that our PSE session is a contrived situation. Yes, it might be fabricated, in that we are experimenting with attitudes that might not be the accepted norm to the children. However, at least, through setting up the scheme of PSE, we are ensuring that our children get 35 minutes a week where we all agree to be nice to each other without fear of shame and embarrassment and ridicule, and 35 minutes is better than nothing.'

Taking this view, the hope is that children will be able to explore different styles of living within the supportive framework of their personal and social education lesson. Ideally, it is hoped, the attitudes they are encouraged to develop will transfer to the wider life of school in general and, indeed, to life outside school.

This, then, is the second function of personal and social education: to foster the strategies and knowledge that children need to entitle them to 'enter the world' and feel at ease in their independence. The establishment and maintenance of happy relationships is basic to personal development, as well as knowing how to get on in the world. We all need other people, but it is sometimes very difficult to get on with those other people. This level of helping children to cope with their feelings, and giving them the skills and confidence to be happy with others, is a crucial element.

In addition to the personal development of the individual, personal and social education is also concerned with the accumulation of knowledge of systems and organisations. These, for example, would include a knowledge of the school and its place in the local environment; an awareness of political systems, of other people's codes of conduct, of bureaucracy; a familiarity with customs and traditions; and experience of the world of work.

Detailed consideration is given to the organisation of personal and social education within the school curriculum in section 1B.

Frameworks for personal and social education

As I have already stressed, prescribed schemes of personal and social education are dangerous. No one school's organisation is totally applicable to any other's. A good friend of mine, John A, tells of his disastrous experiences when he was charged with organising personal and social education in his school some years ago. Fired with enthusiasm, he searched other schools' schemes, read extensively, and thought deeply about the matter. He finally produced a masterpiece of a syllabus, a week-by-week, almost a blow-by-blow scheme, in which he detailed content, activity, personnel, and so on. He was, of course, being as helpful as he could to his colleagues, saving them much work and research by presenting it all there for them. He had done the background; all they had to do now was the teaching.

He was greeted by a paper aeroplane soon after the issue of his master-plan as he entered the staffroom. So much for that. John learned the hard way, as do many organisers and curriculum planners, that when it comes to innovation, people, including teachers, have to be persuaded, cajoled, quietly guided into ways of thinking and behaving, rather than hit over the head with ideas, even if those ideas are good for them. Personal and social education is to do with emotions and feelings; its implications for teaching style are unsettling, suggesting that teachers will have to adopt a new methodology. Teachers feel that their traditional role is threatened, and do not quite know how to cope or react. These hesitations are understandable. Equally understandable is the hostile reaction of teachers to schemes that are thrust upon them without warning or due consultation.

John had no alternative but to abandon his master-plan. In fact, his efforts, so well meant, were counterproductive, and gave rise to all sorts of tensions and hostilities in the staffroom. He shelved all attempts to get his schemes off the ground until 18 months later. Then he quietly introduced the idea by chatting informally to colleagues and winning them over. This approach called for a lot more effort and restraint on his part, particularly as he was dedicated to the idea of personal and social education and committed personally to its introduction into his school. The investment was worthwhile. He gradually persuaded colleagues to try out some ideas, and, over the year, involved more and more people in the schemes.

It is certainly dangerous to attempt to impose schemes on the staff. Yet teachers, individually and as staff bodies, actively look for advice on planning their schemes when introducing personal and social education into their curricula. The point is worth remembering by all organisers of such schemes; it is a high-yield dividend in terms of personal development and competence on the part of the pupils and teachers; it merits high-risk investment of time, effort and resources.

So far this book has offered the advice that schools ought to decide for themselves what they consider relevant and meaningful to the needs of their pupils, and to include those aspects into their programmes. Yet this advice is not far-reaching enough for someone who himself has little or no experience of personal and social education, as is often the case in schools. An enthusiastic teacher who has expressed an interest in this area may well find himself in charge of its organisation, even though he has had no guidance in his initial or on-going training.

In an attempt to meet this need, I would refer to the frameworks adopted by a number of schools, and exemplified in the work of Dr Leslie Button (1981) and Jill Baldwin and Harry Wells (1979–1982) (see Bibliography, section 3.1.). The frameworks follow two parameters, or matrices, focusing on (1) areas which are central to the child's development, in terms of acquisition of both skills and knowledge, and (2) periods of time.

The topics that Button has identified as being themes which will have recurrent relevance throughout the child's school life are:
– the pupil's place in the school
– caring community
– relationships, the self and social skills
– communication skills
– academic guidance and careers education
– health and hygiene
– personal interests

The time sequences are arranged to follow the child's chronological progress through school (see illustration opposite).

Planning schedule: year three

Theme	Stage 1	Stage 2	Stage 3	Stage 4	Stage 5	Stage 6
The pupil's place in the school	Ideas for assembly*	Rehearse assembly Prepare third year meeting*	Year meeting – report*			Ideas for assembly*
Caring community	Welcome back. Support-contracts Caring/administration**	Consolidate caring/administration*	Focus on trust and support**	Renew contracts*	Loneliness – action research **	Review caring/administration Loneliness – report*
Relationships the self and social skills				Friendship** Social skills**	Friendship* Social skills workshop**	Social skills workshop***
Communication skills		Public statements – year meeting – personal interests**	Personal conversations – listening and empathy**			
School work and study skills	Academic support groups Review personal objectives*	Academic support groups – review progress*	Review progress in support groups*			Review work of support groups*
Academic guidance and careers education						
Health and hygiene						
Personal interests	Summer holidays – public statements**	Widening personal experience*				Activities for half-term holiday*

* The use of one, two, or three asterisks indicates the emphasis given to a topic within the programme.

In practice, Button's book makes up a coherent scheme of personal and social education, following through the child's total school life. Teachers who adopt the scheme completely will be able to look to a certain time in the books relevant to their specific year group, say, autumn term, week 2, and have immediate ideas and resources for that week's lessons. Aspects which are particularly relevant to a time, say Christmas, or induction into the school, or preparation for work experience, will be asterisked to highlight their importance. There is, for example, an emphasis on study skills in the fourth year, on preparation for work in the fifth, on decision-making skills in the third ready for options, and so on.

These are very useful schemes. Naturally, many teachers are resistant to the idea of having it all carefully laid out for them, thinking that this might be imposition; many organisers are worried that teachers will 'teach from the book'. This anxiety has very real foundations; personal and social education is anything but a mechanical activity that can be taught through any book. Its value is in the educational process, the fact that teachers and pupils are sharing together a first-hand experience. A book must never come between teacher and pupils: it is the medium but not the process. While a book is an invaluable resource for ideas and inspiration, the most valuable resource for learning is the children themselves.

Because personal and social education is to do with reality, not an abstraction of it as is so often true of many traditional curriculum areas, it must be regarded as dynamic. A scheme must never become static. Staff must never feel that they now have the answer for the next five years. They should constantly review and modify their practice. Perhaps frameworks might remain stable for a period of time, but slots within those frameworks are constantly under revision, simply to meet the needs for which they were designed – the needs of the children within any given situation. Of course, this demands close liaison and discussion among the people engaged in a scheme. The very organisation of personal and social education in a school requires strong communication links, and the process of organisation and teaching becomes an educational experience for the teachers.

In this section we have looked at one of the major difficulties facing secondary schools, that it is very much an individual choice left to schools to decide their own criteria in managing schemes of personal and social education. Current literature tends to be couched in terms of abstraction that are difficult to put into practice. There is plenty of good common-sense advice available that personal and social education ought to be on schools' curricula, and why; but there is little offered in the way of translating that abstraction into real class practice. For example, we know from the literature that personal and social education is a powerful factor for change in society, yet there is little guidance as to what criteria we ought to adopt to say that personal development has taken place. What happens when children and teachers become involved in personal and social education? Does it have any lasting effects?

These and many more questions need answering. There should be more research and more practical guidance for teachers attempting to implement schemes. There is enormous scope for research into the nature of personal development and the contribution made by personal and social education in the school curriculum.

In the next section we shall look in depth at the difficult question that we have touched upon in this section: where does personal and social education feature in school life, and how and to what extent is it incorporated into the curriculum? Or is it an all-pervading attitude throughout the school?

B

The Way In:
personal and social
education
and the curriculum

In this section we shall look at the integration of personal and social education into the whole curriculum. It is a difficult problem, and opinions are often divided among teachers as to where it belongs.

Before they can decide where to put personal and social education on their curricula, schools need to answer many questions, which will surely include the following:

1 Is personal and social education a subject or a set of attitudes?
2 Does it qualify for legitimate timetabling, or should it be picked up at random?
3 Should it be presented as a consciously organised scheme or should its presentation be 'inspirational'?
4 Is it imparted through specific teaching methodologies and learning strategies, or through example?
5 Is it to be taught by everyone on the staff or just by those who are committed?
6 Is every teacher a pastoral tutor, or just those who have the necessary skills and inclinations?

Sometimes opinion is divided among school staff as to what they should be doing and how they should be doing it (and frequently *who* should be doing it) but no staff should let such discussions stand in the way of somebody actually doing it.

The following sections attempt to offer some frameworks and models for schools to consider. It must be emphasised that these models are *only* 'ways in'. The origins of any scheme of personal and social education becomes less and less obvious as time goes on and the scheme develops. They are not permanent models, but just some ideas on how to start.

Competence and performance: a theory of personal and social adequacy

At this point it might be useful to mention a theory I have developed while engaged in my own research in personal and social education. I work with many teachers and pupils while assisting schools in setting up their schemes, and my own research is firmly rooted in the everyday practice of school life. In trying to clarify my own views as to the nature of personal development, I came to the conclusion that children and teachers operate on at least two levels of commitment. These levels I have termed 'competence' and 'performance'. I borrowed these terms from Noam Chomsky, an eminent thinker in the field of linguistics, who used them to describe two levels of language development and use. In *Aspects of the Theory of Syntax* (MIT, 1964) Chomsky comments:

> We thus make a fundamental distinction between competence (the speaker-hearer's knowledge of his language), and performance (the actual use of language in concrete situations).

Applying the notions of competence and performance to the development of personal adequacy, I feel it is possible for a learner to become skilled at a superficial level (performance) without accepting what he is doing as a moral code (competence). In terms of the aims of education, a performance level is insufficient to produce a morally educated person.

In similar vein, Stanton *et al* (1980) point to the development of skills on a hierarchical basis:

> It may be important to distinguish between (a) relatively simple skills, (b) compound (or complex) skills, and (c) the ability to deploy a compound skill.
>
> For example,
>
> (a) steering ⟶ (b) riding a bike ⟶ (c) riding safely in traffic
>
> A 'compound skill', such as riding a bike, is more than a collection of simple skills. Its development may still, however, only require well-organised practice.

Wilson *et al* (1967) also point to the cumulative development of increasingly complex skills in driving a car, skills ranging through 'factual information (where the brake and accelerator are), rules of thumb (Don't switch on when in gear), and practice'.

But skills of a mechanical nature, suggest Stanton *et al* and Wilson *et al* are subsidiary elements within the total exercise of being a safe driver. The good road user, they suggest, will have learnt the skills of negotiating traffic, will have accepted the responsibility of being a road user, and will have regard for other road users.

In their characterisation of the morally educated person, Wilson *et al* point to those aspects of *responsibility* and *regard*, which are themselves dependent on the person's *rationality*. Responsibility and regard may be taught, but not necessarily learnt, or put into practice. For values to be realised in practice, there must be an initial *intentionality*.

We might be tempted to say that we can divide the task of moral education into two parts. First we should educate people so as to give them the skills, abilities and knowledge required for moral decisions: . . . and then we should 'give them the motivation' to put these into practice. (Wilson *et al*, 1967, p. 97)

Motivation alone, however, does not of itself lead to competence. A learner could demonstrate his interpersonal skills for all sorts of reasons – personal enrichment, reward, fear of punishment – without actually having accepted the values of what he is doing. 'This would not make them into more reasonable people, and would not count as education,' concludes Wilson. 'We need rather some way of educating . . . people so as to improve this deep and subtle form of rationality.'

My views of the aims of personal and social education have led me to look for strategies to develop the competence of the learner. We do this first by teaching actively for performance, a skills-level adequacy that is going to help children enormously in coping with the world and their own development. Many children will stop at the level of performance. They may well accept certain skills and accumulate certain packets of knowledge that will help them through life, without necessarily developing appropriate accompanying attitudes. For example, I am reminded that Tom and Barry, two of my fourth-year pupils, improved their social skills so much under my guidance, that they found they could refine their stealing strategies dramatically. Tom would distract the shopkeeper with his newly-found conversation skills while Barry stole goods from the stands outside the shop. Their performance skills were developing nicely; the grasp of moral values was far behind. Tom's mother told me later that the magistrates commended her on having such a well-mannered, well-spoken son. I had been very successful in teaching social skills to the boys at a performance level; I had not been so good at persuading them of the necessity for developing an appropriate moral code. I had, in fact, produced two first-rate con-men.

Models of the organisation of personal and social education in secondary schools

Given that ultimately we are teaching for a personal commitment by children to a code of living which is right for them and for society in general (competence), on an everyday, practical level we are aiming for the development of attitudes and knowledge that are going to assist children in their daily life and on their entry to the world outside school (performance).

If we focus on performance as a skills-level approach, we can identify two different aspects that we teach for in personal and social education:

1 the development of attitudes and behaviours appropriate to living in society and to the development of the individual;
2 the acquisition of knowledge and understanding of systems and organisations appropriate to the child's well-being in school and in the world at large.

According to current literature, to achieve this involves consciously developing the qualities of self-confidence, self-organisation, group co-operation, responsibility, and independence in our children. Our active input in personal and social education will identify those areas where we, as tutors and supervisors, may actively assist in the development of these qualities. Having identified the areas, we then, as already indicated in section 1A, accelerate the process. We focus on aspects which we consider through our professional judgement, and in consultation with colleagues and children, to be relevant and meaningful, and we accelerate the 'internalisation process', the way in which children see the value of what they are learning and decide for themselves if they wish to accept it.

It is likely that schools will see their organisation in more than one of the models presented below. Most school organisation is eclectic in nature, and, although they might take aspects of the models as appropriate to themselves, there is broad overlap of many aspects and issues suggested here.

Model 1: a framework for the whole school curriculum

This approach sees personal and social education as constituting the background to the whole curriculum. Approaches and attitudes through all areas of the curriculum stress the notions of care and support. Academic/vocational lessons are taught with regard to the child's welfare and all teachers regard themselves as having pastoral responsibility and are prepared to act as counsellors and welfare agents.

Schools following this model may well feel that, as appropriate values and attitudes are already so well established, personal and social education is unnecessary. Perhaps they see any specific input as a reinforcement of already established attitudes, or as a time to impart specific knowledge about, for example, health education, or work in the local community, or pet welfare.

I certainly recommend that personal and social education acts as a foundation for the curriculum in terms of attitudes. This is what many schools maintain as crucial to their stated aims and objectives. It seems rather dangerous, however, to assume that personal and social education is in practice on this 'inspirational' basis without some sort of monitoring process going on.

The foundation of personal and social education is in the dynamism of the educational process. If pastoral aspects of the school are conducted on a random basis, then not all children are going to benefit as thoroughly as they might have, had the pastoral curriculum been structured. I mentioned earlier that the children in our schools will certainly cope without tutors and supervisors; but if their supervisors can successfully identify their areas of need, imagine a solution to those needs, and accelerate the process by putting the solutions into practice, then the children will cope much more successfully. Teachers who assume that the children will 'learn by example' or 'pick it up as they go along' do their children a disservice. Certainly, a total framework of care and support is an ideal to be aimed for, but we need to ensure also a specific input for the areas of uncertainty.

Model 2: through form tutors

This approach presupposes that a tutorial system already operates in the school, alongside the academic organisation. The two systems might be parallel, complementary or integrative.

Parallel

The tutorial system would run concurrent with the academic, having equal status in terms of resources, staffing and credibility. They would, however, be seen as separate elements of the curriculum. The role of tutor might not be equated with the role of teacher. Aspects touched on in the pastoral system may well have no place within the academic system.

Complementary

The tutorial and academic systems would work together in harmony, yet both be seen as separate entities. Aspects of pastoral work would receive attention in the academic life of the school and vice versa. Teachers would have to assume their role as pastoral tutors at appropriate points in the day. There is probably less danger of conflict of roles in this scheme.

Integrative

In this system the edges blur and sometimes disappear altogether, where pastoral elements are taught through the medium of academic subjects. The danger in this system is that the academic and tutorial systems tend to be so closely integrated that confusion might arise as to who is doing what and to whom. Clearly this arrangement calls for close liaison and careful planning by all staff engaged in the process.

The strength of this model is that each and every child receives personal support, active care from a certain individual with whom they can identify and to whom they can go in time of trouble. Its weakness is that the form tutors may well sometimes feel isolated and in need of personal support themselves. They will need guidance in content areas to be covered in personal and social education sessions, and for this regular, scheduled meetings must be arranged.

The tutorial systems need to operate efficiently, both in terms of personnel and their various job specifications, and in terms of planning for the term's or year's programme. Communication channels must be open at all times, and a feeling of team spirit must secure an easy and happy exchange at all levels, from headteacher down to class tutor; then this can be a very powerful approach.

Model 3: through religious education

This approach sees religious education as an aspect of the academic curriculum, but the only area that deals specifically with issues of personal and social education. Most teachers would probably agree that personal and social education can be equated in many respects with religious education in conveying attitudes, skills and knowledge that will enable children to adapt to the world more efficiently. Both disciplines are concerned with aiming for a society of morally educated people: that is, people who have regard for other people as well as for themselves; who appreciate their personal responsibilities as individuals living in a society of other individuals; and who have the wisdom to apply their regard and responsibility with a clear intention.

Colleagues with whom I have worked have commented that they see personal and social education as 'religion through the back door'. I take no issue with this. I believe that education is to do with love, and both religious education and personal and social education emphasise the quality of love. Personal religion is about belief in an own God or Gods. Personal and social education may be an alternative means of encouraging children to develop attitudes or behaviour which have much in common with how good people should behave towards themselves and others.

In terms of a school's organisation, to focus only on religious education, or indeed any one curriculum area, as the vehicle of personal and social education is wasteful of resources and limiting on at least two counts: in the scope of personal and social education, and of the role of the school. In its social function of the accumulation of specific knowledge, personal and social education is much broader in its focus than simply instruction in codes of morality. In addition, in terms of staffing, this approach is restrictive, assigning teachers to the role of academic instructors and the school to that of an academic institution instead of a total caring community.

Model 4: through health and sex education

It is interesting how personal and social education was once seen as an aspect of health education, and now the wheel is turning so that health education is seen as part of personal and social education.

Many schools still base their schemes of personal and social education within health and sex education. This approach is based in the academic curriculum, and again places a heavy emphasis on attitudes as content. Much attention is paid to the overt teaching of moral codes and ethics. This approach draws heavily on the resources of religious education, parentcraft and allied subjects. It is in areas of the curriculum like these that the relevance of personal and social education is immediately apparent, because those areas are to do with relationships, feelings and the implications of the development of personal and social adequacy. Before we can get on to the detail of health and sex education in terms of practical knowledge and interpersonal skills, we need to develop caring attitudes among the children.

In our class practice we have to establish the right atmosphere for the teaching and learning of the knowledge aspects of health and sex education. This atmosphere will stress the need for children to respect each other, to listen and learn with compassion and sensitivity, to understand that we are talking about real matters of feelings and emotions. Children easily wound each other by thoughtless remarks, and the establishment of the right atmosphere will guard against any possible embarrassment or hurt by giggling or inappropriate behaviour.

They also need to be aware of the need for stable relationships as a firm foundation to family life and personal fulfilment. These are the aspects that health and sex education are trying to impart, and the educational process in class is an initial mirrored experience of what the children might encounter in their developing personal relationships.

Model 5: through integrated studies

This approach takes a global view of the curriculum, and has as its core the school ethic of a caring community. Much interdisciplinary work is encouraged, with a deliberate overlap between pastoral and academic organisations and contents, and with overlap between academic departments. Staff see themselves as academic subject teachers and as pastoral tutors, and the school management ethos should certainly encourage this view. Team teaching may well be an organisational necessity.

The strength of this approach is its involvement of academic departments in what is usually seen as pastoral territory, and an integration of the academic life of the school through pastoral measures. Areas that would probably take a vigorous lead would be humanities or civics or the departments of social education that are increasingly being founded in schools. Many schools, in fact, are re-defining and re-naming many of the traditional departments within humanities; 'civics' or 'sociology' or other named departments either integrate with, become absorbed into, or change altogether into departments of social education. The possible weaknesses of the approach are the overwhelming need for good communication systems, discussed above, and the possible eclipse of the form tutor.

Children in organisations need to be able to identify with a trusted adult in whom they may confide and to whom they may go in time of trouble. No doubt any school that had the vision to have a coherent, integrated approach to personal and social education would also see the need for a tutorial system, so the position of form tutor would still have its true importance. But in this approach the lead-in would be through a system of integrated studies rather than through the direct intervention of the form tutor.

Model 6: through careers education

When the notion of careers education was first introduced it was defined as preparing the pupil for finding a job. The work undertaken in a traditional careers department was probably seen in employment-oriented terms: the head of department or careers teacher was tradition-ally viewed as the prime agent who negotiated the jobs for the school-leavers. As in many cases, the function and the nature of educational areas have changed to meet the rapidly shifting needs of young people. Because of the changing face of society and of the changing employment situation, the perception of 'careers' has changed. Our present definition of careers is changing to meet its widening function and to attempt to describe more accurately the process of preparing young people for adult life.

Certainly schools are aware of their responsibility in preparing youngsters for employment. The traditional careers department no doubt involves itself in schemes of work experience, is closely associated with industry and commerce, has close links with and support from careers agencies and youth employment offices. Many schools are adopting schemes of vocational studies, along with traditional academic studies. Schemes such as the National Technical and Vocational Education Initiative (NTVEI) are gaining credibility within the secondary sector as being an educational factor that is aiming for direct relevance to the needs of young people. It is very early days yet to attempt an assessment of such schemes, but some NTVEI schemes do not appear to offer the balance and breadth essential in a rapidly changing economy and labour market. There are dangers in early specialisation and the search for 'relevance' could lead to a narrowly conceived utilitarian approach to education.

Initiatives such as an integrated curriculum across the 14–19 age range are also indicative of the need, seen at national as well as local level, of using school as a practice ground for when the young people have to stand on their own feet in work and in society at large.

Because of the dual nature and responsibilities of a specific preparation for employment and a general preparation for life after school, many schools are organising their careers education as a two-tier system. The structure could be seen as:

1 Careers = finding a job. Most of this work is seen in the traditional sense of specific preparation for employment. It is centred around the fourth and fifth years in secondary schools or in the sixth form. Many schools, however, are starting careers education in the third year, and certainly there is generally much preparation in the third year in choosing options. That preparation itself would have had a strong focus in personal and social education sessions on decision-making and study skills, as well as much group work to establish the need for co-operation and group interrelationships.

2 Careers = preparation for the world outside school. This work is focused directly on personal and social education, involving decision-making, self-awareness, and the pupils' knowledge of their own potential. Much emphasis would be laid on an awareness of systems, such as opportunities for continuing education, schemes of work experience, preparation for leisure. There is no standard 'point of entry' in the school's chronology. The point of entry is determined as part of school policy regulating the incorporation of personal and social education. Systematic training could be provided from year 1, or there could be a blitz programme in year 5. It all depends on the identified needs of the individual school.

In view of the changing definition of careers education, staff often feel unsure as to how far they should take their involvement in preparing youngsters for a world of work or for a world of unemployment. With the changing employment scene, with the likelihood of greater leisure time and facilities earlier in life, schools find themselves with the responsibility of education for that particular social need. The work ethic no longer applies as much as before, either as an incentive in schools for conscientious application, or as an ultimate objective for life after school. The implications are far-reaching and relevant to all areas of school life. What price examinations, for example? Is a traditional method of assessment through formal examinations appropriate to current vocational needs? Or would a system of profiling be more appropriate, an on-going system of assessment in personal as well as academic achievement? (see p 133) These and many other questions need to be considered carefully by schools in determining their policies of careers education.

The models offered here are reflective of much current practice in schools. What is certain is that there is an overwhelming need for a clear policy for the development of a pastoral curriculum. That point must never be overlooked. Exactly which department or agency takes the lead in organising personal and social education in the school, or accepting the focus for personal and social education, is up to the individual school policy-makers. Schools that still operate on an 'inspirational' basis, hoping that there will be a general reflection of care and support in the school, but without making adequate provision for its specific inclusion in the curriculum, are advocating a head-in-the-sand approach to the aims of education.

A final word of advice to organisers of personal and social education in schools is never be afraid of abandoning any one scheme if it does not work. Try out another, and another if necessary, until the right one is found to meet your needs.

C

Anxieties and constraints of teachers involved in schemes of personal and social education

When schools first decide to publish their intentions of rationalising their schemes of personal and social education, a number of teachers often feel rather anxious. Already in the short time that personal and social education has been around in a 'public' form, a certain mythology has grown up around it. Teachers have the impression that the whole area is not quite respectable. It is to the academic curriculum as alternative medicine is to drugs: not quite scientific and imbued with a bit of chicanery.

I have presented below some of the objections that are frequently raised by teachers when they are first involved in schemes of personal and social education. The purpose of this section is to allay these fears, and to show that personal and social education is a modern, efficient way of helping youngsters to help themselves, and definitely a non-threatening exercise. It is certainly challenging and stimulating; to that extent it is provocative, in that anything that causes turbulence is going to rock a few stable boats. But personal and social education is neither mysterious nor mystical: it is exciting, dynamic and, most of all, fun.

Statement one: 'But I already do this in my lessons'

Many teachers experience a feeling of *déjà vu* when they become involved in a scheme of personal and social education. When methodologies are demonstrated and contents explained, teachers often claim that they already do that in their lessons.

They are absolutely right. Good teachers have always been aware of their class practice, looking critically at what they are doing even as they do it; they have always been aware that they are teaching children primarily and teaching subjects secondarily; they intuitively react to changes in the class atmosphere and introduce new stimuli or pace at the right time, because they have developed a wide, sensitive repertoire of teaching skills and techniques.

Perhaps good teachers are born, but with further training to refine their expertise they can become excellent teachers. The greater the skill and involvement and repertoire of teachers, the more they will enhance the quality of education for the children in their care. None of us should ever believe that we have it made and no longer need any further training. The educational experience in schools is often as much a learning experience for the teachers as for the children they teach.

Another point to remember is that not all children are going to benefit from one teacher's classes. Most teachers meet only a proportion of the children in the school. Those children who do not meet that particular teacher may meet someone less experienced or gifted. It is then certainly in everybody's interests that the school has a well-defined policy which includes a systematic input of in-service support, (see sections 3C and 4B). If all staff are prepared to learn from and help each other, the atmosphere is vastly enhanced and a tremendous spirit of team co-operation may be developed.

It is true that many teachers are already practising personal and social education in their traditional academic lessons. Some subjects such as drama and religious education clearly have affinities with personal and social education in delivery and content. They are concerned with the personal development of the pupil, strengthening co-operative links with other pupils, stressing the need for the development of interpersonal skills. Activities such as group work, discussion, questionnaires, role-play and so on, which are applicable to active personal and social education are the cornerstones of such lessons.

It is precisely this point that is powerful in its implications for the total curriculum: that methodologies and strategies which strengthen the relationships and activities highlighted in personal and social education are equally applicable across the board. It is as easy and appropriate to practise group work and communication exercises in mathematics and geography. Viewed in this way we can go the full cycle and say that attitudes conveyed through teaching and learning styles may be exercised in any of the traditional curriculum areas.

I have stated above that personal and social education is more about the process of learning than the content of the lesson. The same can obviously be true in conveying attitudes and values through the academic curriculum. Perhaps certain lessons rely heavily on an instructional component, but there is still a personal and social educational component going on through the process of the lesson. This distinction is worth bearing in mind. The case in many secondary schools is that much emphasis is laid on instruction in terms of knowledge/content, and on teaching style. For those of us who practise an instructional style, methodologies appropriate to personal and social education will perhaps be alien and challenging. But for those of us who are already engaged in an educational style which focuses on the child as the subject of education rather than on the content of a subject-matter, then the statement of 'But I already do this in my lessons' is quite right. Long may it continue!

Statement two: 'I am trained to teach maths. Don't tell me to be a surrogate parent or a welfare worker. I feel comfortable with maths.'

Colleagues who attempt to take refuge in their specialised disciplines must be respected in their views, since most traditional initial teacher-training lays almost exclusive emphasis on teaching the subject, although students are given a cursory training in the 'disciplines' of education, in its philosophy, psychology and sociology. These disciplines, however, are useless when a teacher is faced with the problem of how to get 5B through their O-levels to their parents' satisfaction. Practical help is to be found in the growing literature of Action Research in following through the new movement of educational research (see bibliography). Perhaps schools are overly concerned with instructional activities, so threatened and overwhelmed are we by examinations, accountability, curricular constraints.

The teacher who hesitates in wondering to what extent he is responsible for the child's welfare is wise. To what extent should schools accept the responsibility of the child's moral, emotional and spiritual welfare? What happened to the parents? What right have schools to interfere? The law tells us that we must act as responsible adults, *in loco parentis*, but *in loco* suggests 'in their absence', not 'as their surrogates'.

Yet the concept of education has a notional value of widening experience. *Ex duco* implies just that: 'I lead out' rather than 'I put in'. Education is not only instruction. The new educational wave of which personal and social education is the focus demands that teachers accept the responsibility of the child's education as well as his instruction. If education implies that we teach the children to think, then we must be ready to let them think, to guide their thinking, to arrange their environments to encourage them to think for themselves and not necessarily copy the thoughts of their teachers.

This means that in order to educate children to cope in today's world, teachers have no choice but to accept a pastoral role as well as a traditionally acceptable instructional role. This necessity is highlighted by two factors:

1 The increasing demands of society that schools should accept this function. With traditional institutions of the family, the church, the concept of stable relationships crumbling around their ears, where do young people turn as the only stable point of reference in their lives? Their teachers who, no matter what you do to them, will always be there. Schools have to take on the responsibility, simply

because there is no one else.

2 The takeover by the microchip. In an increasingly technological society, teachers have to come to terms with the fact that modern technology can often instruct more efficiently than they can. Instead of trying to beat computers at their own game, teachers can now adapt to a school environment where they are freed to get on with the job of educating, and leave much of the rote nature of instruction to the machines.

Gone are the days when the comment of 'Leave me alone to teach maths' was legitimate. Teachers must now accept a wider function in the school. This and further points will be elaborated in section 4 'The changing role of the teacher'.

Statement three: 'I cannot teach personal and social education. I have no idea where to start.'

Two of the greatest constraints on teachers who are invited to embark on a scheme of personal and social education are ignorance and fear: ignorance of what to do and how to do it, and fear of having a go. Many established teachers feel that they are too long in the tooth for this new-fangled business. Nothing could be further from the truth. Many teachers have long acted on an intuitive basis in terms of pastoral work. Counselling, for example, is a new name for a very old-established activity: that of listening carefully and sympathetically to other people. Many teachers would be surprised to hear themselves termed 'skilled counsellors'; they would probably describe themselves as 'good listeners'.

Discipline, a very old-fashioned notion, is at the very heart of personal and social education. A firm, friendly relationship in class, where the pupils are in no doubt that their teacher is acting in their very best interests, is of paramount importance.

Long-established educational notions of care and support are as relevant today as they ever were. The difference is, perhaps, that teachers are encouraged to develop awareness and insight into what they are doing so that they may widen their scope in two ways: first, to show their care and support more efficiently, through developing their interpersonal expertise; secondly, to pass on those skills to the children so that they may care for each other.

The nature of personal and social education is that it is a co-operative exercise, a social activity. Traditionally, all activity and traffic of conventional lessons is guided through the teacher, who is in unilateral control. In the practice of personal and social education the teacher sometimes deflects the action from himself or herself; instead of being the central agent to show concern he or she will involve the children in caring for each other. Certainly there are many times and places for a one-to-one relationship between teacher and pupil; but personal and social education strategies also call for the teacher's involving other pupils in the social process. He or she will encourage children to listen to each other, and deliberately teach them how to do so.

These are skills which can easily be learnt. At present there is not enough systematic guidance in our initial teacher-training institutions. Most training of established, experienced teachers is in an in-service mode. This support is of paramount importance, for without it schemes may well not get off the ground as effectively as they might.

More will be said on this matter in section 4B 'Support', but I will here make an initial plea to all Local Education Authorities to give due priority to in-service support, and support of a correct nature. The investment is well worthwhile.

Statement four: 'In personal and social education we are teaching the children values. We ought not to be teaching values; that is brainwashing.'

This is a fear voiced by many teachers, and, to my mind, is quite unnecessary. I do appreciate that teachers are extremely reasonable people who are prepared to take every precaution not to impose their own ideas on the children.

I would respond to the fear of teaching 'values' in two ways:

1 In many ways, through the processes of personal and social education, the exercise is a liberating activity rather than a restrictive one.

2 Yes, we are teaching values. Let us accept the fact, only let us agree to the values to be taught.

To expand these notions:

1 *Personal and social education as a liberating exercise*

It is very easy to teach children which decisions to make. We could take any choice – say whether to read an adventure or a science-fiction book, or whether to watch television first or do our homework – and point out the merits and demerits in the choice. How much more difficult it is to teach our children *how* to make decisions. Here we abandon any preconceptions of our own as to which choice we feel the children ought to make, and we concentrate on the process of making the decision. A decision-making process puts the responsibility on the children to make their own appropriate choice, and the responsibility on us to help them through the process of making decisions.

2 *Yes, we are teaching values*

Teachers worry about 'imposing middle-class values' on their pupils. I feel this worry is without foundation. In schools we have already decided on our values system; it is there for all to see in our curriculum, in our stated aims and objectives, in the appearance and behaviour of our staff body. Our values are no secret.

What we need to ensure is that a framework for our values is fully agreed by all members of staff, and practised. It is not possible for all values to be agreed by all teachers; we live in a pluralist society, and one of our educational aims is to develop understanding and tolerance of the varied cultures and beliefs in our society and in any school.

It is acceptable for teachers to promote those values on which there is consensus, for example, 'Thou shalt not kill'; it is not acceptable in areas of controversy, for example, noise pollution or conservation. If those agreed values are promoted with sincerity and conviction, then teachers' fears are without foundation. Our society is founded on certain values, on democracy and compassion. Those values single it out from many other societies where oppression and dictatorship are the ruling values. If we can impart these values to the children who are going to be the future citizens of that society, then we shall have fulfilled our agreed aims of education.

Statement five: 'Personal and social education is to do with relationships. You cannot teach relationships.'

This view is often voiced by colleagues and seems based on two assumptions; first, that we cannot actively assist in enhancing areas like relationships, and second, that relationships maintain a certain status quo and do not require working at. This is a rather naïve view of people's abilities to live at peace with one another. Relationships do not simply happen. They are formed through an initial contact, and then maintained with effort or allowed to decline.

The problem for teachers seems to be two-fold here. It is again a 'content or process' dilemma. If we are to teach relationships, ask colleagues, what are we supposed to be teaching? Does this mean that we all have to be friends all the time? What about social misfits, sworn enemies, children with emotional difficulties? What about the relationship between teachers and the children? Secondly, how do we teach relationships? It is an emotive area; it is to do with people's feelings for each other. How do we teach that?

School is a place for forming relationships in at least two distinct senses. First, it is a place where children may form friendships or acquaintanceships – relationships of various levels of intimacy and trust. Secondly, it is a practice ground for forming and maintaining relationships, and for gaining the wisdom to know when not to get too involved or when to break the friendship off. This would include practising the skill of handling arguments and disagreements, or how to avoid conflict, while still keeping one's own integrity and self-respect. This is a very wide area, and it must be decided through discussion with colleagues which aspects should be attempted within the pastoral syllabus. Colleagues may feel that three areas require attention throughout the child's school life; those of relationships with family, with peers, and with adults including figures of authority.

Perhaps the first task when the children join the school would be to help them to get to know each other and to establish a working basis of trust and mutual respect. By the fifth year we would be looking at aspects of life after school; working with colleagues; planning for lasting friendships, including marriage; accepting responsibility. If we can actively work towards helping children to recognise and cope with relationships, to avoid crises, and to deal with difficulties when they arise, as they surely will, then we are helping our children to develop the complex skills of getting on with other people and living a happy life of self-fulfilment. So many of our young people undervalue themselves, have a poor self-image, accept that they are worthy only of criticism and not of love. We can help them out of that syndrome into a life of greater strength and happiness.

It can all begin in the real life of class, where we can draw on the first hand experience of forming friendships with each other. The first thing that has to be done is to establish an agreed supportive atmosphere. If we can all contract in to the agreed atmosphere of trust, then no one need fear rebuff or ridicule at letting their guard slip. From there we can engage in a multitude of exercises: trust exercises, quizzes, question-naires, and so on. The focus of any of these exercises is the child; everything is couched in terms relevant to him or her, so that he or she can experience it personally.

For example:
- a 'life space' diagram (see Button, 1981) looks at ME in relation to other people

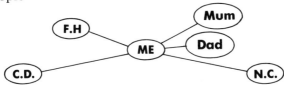

- a questionnaire talks about ME

Me as I see me   +   −
1 I get on well with others   3 2 1   1 2 3
2 I am a good friend   3 2 1   1 2 3
3 I like myself   3 2 1   1 2 3

- a situation that talks about ME

You are at a party and your boyfriend starts dancing with another girl. Do you:
1 go home?
2 walk up and say, 'Excuse me. You're with me'?
3 dance with another boy?

Today industry is recognising the value of social skills, and many companies have trained personnel on hand to help employees to keep a harmonious atmosphere conducive to good labour relations and high productivity. Marriage guidance and other professional counsellors do the same, helping people to look at themselves and at other people close to them, and cope with difficulties. So if sometimes, as adults, we need help to live with other people, why should children be different?

In my opinion, with our intervention as teachers, we can look to a future society with fewer divorces, less baby-bashing, and a far more positive outlook. True, it will take a long time, but it will happen. We are educating tomorrow's adults who will in turn educate their children. The chain starts with us.

Statement six: 'If I engage in this sort of practice, my authority will be undermined.'

Many colleagues feel that if they encourage a democratic relationship in their classes, that children have a say in determining what goes on in class, in directing activity, in accepting the responsibility for their own learning, then their authority as teachers will be eroded. This anxiety makes people suspicious of personal and social education, feeling sometimes that it could be a potentially subversive activity. It is all right, they feel, for social workers or youth agencies to encourage that sort of liberal, unstructured atmosphere, but not at all appropriate for school practice.

Perhaps this apprehension is caused by a confusion about the meaning of democracy, and about the meaning of leadership. There are different forms of democracy, and different styles of leadership; and provided teachers adopt appropriate management strategies such as a dynamic leadership that encourages a democratic relationship among the children, they will find that their natural authority is enhanced rather than undermined. (For a more detailed discussion about styles of leadership, see p. 62.)

Very often, when teachers first start exploring methodologies that encourage children to talk to each other and to trust each other, they find that they of necessity must become less central to class involvement, and more diplomatic in guiding the direction of the children's activity. For example, unacceptable behaviour which, in 'conventional' classroom style would be corrected by outright disapproval by the teacher, would be handled by an investigation as to why the child was behaving in such a way; asking the child to examine his or her own behaviour and see why and if he or she should reject it.

Through the practice of personal and social education, elements of vigorous yet considerate leadership emerge; we learn ourselves, as teachers, how to control and manage social situations easily and fluently.

The experience takes practice, and confidence grows with continued practice. It does not happen immediately. What is needed, in terms of support, is intensive initial training in methodologies appropriate to personal and social education, based in class practice, and on-going personalised support to teachers who are experimenting and learning these skills of class management.

Statement seven: 'People expect certain conduct of me as a teacher. I cannot break out of the mould of a traditional teacher to be the sort of teacher that personal and social education requires me to be.'

One of the greatest constraints on teachers is the expectations of other people. Teachers are somehow expected to be all things to all people. They are subject to the approval or disapproval of children, parents, governors, the media, as well as other colleagues. The person they sometimes find it most difficult to be is themselves.

Perhaps the problem is that our most popular image of the teacher is that of the 'authoritarian disciplinarian'. The popular image of school presented through the media is still that of a traditional classroom full of ranked desks and controlled by an omnipotent teacher.

Teachers' images of themselves tend to be self-perpetuating. So often the pattern of life for teachers is their own schooldays → institutions of education → teaching practice school → probationary year; colleagues who break out of this traditional pattern are in the minority. Few teachers arrive out of industry and commerce, or have experience of professions other than teaching, or have experience of groups other than children.

This self-image needs to alter radically. We need to get rid of a 'chalk and talk' image and get to grips with today's society. I am not advocating any trendy movement, but I am recommending an awareness and an alertness to current social and technological as well as educational issues. This awareness could be brought about in many ways, and one of the methods would be a release system built into teachers' contracts to involve them for a short duration, say a year, in other professions and systems. In-service courses could include aspects of management, as well as more conventional educational issues, since strategies of management are as applicable to the classroom as they are to the shop floor.

An altered self-image could affect class practice in schools. It is sad that even today teachers' professional capacity is judged in terms of how well they 'keep control' in a classroom. If teachers can grow professionally and allow their natural instincts to flourish rather than other people's prejudices, then their class practice will also flourish. They will work more as educators and less as instructors. A fuller discussion is found in section 4A 'The changing role of the teacher'.

PART 2

Good Practice

A

Teaching styles

The purpose of describing different teaching styles is that teachers may be aware of at least two things:

1 That it is in everyone's interest that teachers have as wide a professional repertoire as possible; that they are competent in different skills and can switch readily and fluently from one skill to another.

2 That each learning situation demands an appropriate teaching style. If teachers can identify the needs of the children in that particular situation, they can then accommodate those needs by selecting the appropriate accompanying teaching style.

Whichever teaching arrangement we choose will focus not only on how we present our subject matter, but also on how we arrange the conditions of learning. We could perhaps even say that what the pupils learn, and how they learn it, will depend on the arrangement of the learning situation itself.

Experiential learning and knowledge-based learning

The traditional advice offered to teachers when deciding on their practice in class is to determine their objectives. Objectives are seen in terms of specific goals; items to be learnt, behaviours to be adopted, attitudes to be displayed.

This book cannot offer that advice, because personal and social education does not deal so much in pre-specified objectives as in *outcomes*. In a conventional subject-based lesson I can legitimately claim, 'By the end of the lesson the children should be able to do X and Y, that they couldn't do before'. I might even hope, 'By the end of the lesson the children will have learnt X and Y'.

In personal and social education teachers may more appropriately claim, 'In this lesson I am aiming to cover this area and introduce these ideas. I anticipate certain outcomes, but these are general expectations rather than specific objectives'.

In recognising that we need to apply different teaching approaches to different learning situations, we are highlighting an awareness that there are different types of learning. In establishing what they want their pupils to have achieved at the end of their lessons (or series of lessons) teachers must also establish how this should be achieved, that is, what teaching strategies should be employed and what teaching skills are needed for this to come about.

Subjects which are knowledge-based could legitimately be couched in instructional terms, but subjects which are skills/attitudes based are best presented in experiential terms. For personal and social education our strategies should be designed to encourage learning by the pupil through first-hand experience, rather than to focus on an instructional mode, whereby pupils have only a vicarious experience of concepts, skills and attitudes.

Let us take the example of arithmetic. This can be seen in an abstract form of numerical computation, or it can be seen in an applied form of making the weekly budget balance. In the classroom it may be studied in both ways. In its knowledge-based aspect, in practising the methods of mathematics – addition, substraction, multiplication, and so on – we may present it as an abstract concept. We would set the children practical tasks in straightforward sums. If we want to look at arithmetic in its applied sense, then we would introduce real experiences in which it is necessary to use the principles of arithmetic. We would get the children to draw up weekly shopping lists, or tally weekly attendance totals, or run the school bank.

This concept of different strategies for different approaches to learning is outlined in the following model:

A model of teaching strategies

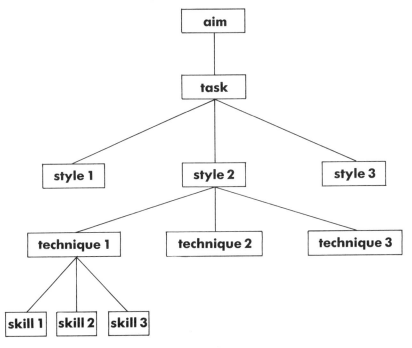

Translated into real teaching terms, this could result in the following outlines:

Strategy 1

Aim	Learners should practise decision-making skills.
Task	From a written passage posing a problem learners are to decide which solution to suggest to solve the problem.
Teaching style	Didactic/instructional
Techniques	1 Teacher distributes papers on which the passage is written.
	2 Teacher instructs the learners to read the passage and answer the questions.
Skills	1 Clarity of instruction.
	2 Organisation of material and learners.
	3 Suggestions, possibly, of how to make the decision.

Strategy 2

Aim	Learners should practise decision-making skills.
Task	From an ostensive, simulated situation posing a problem, learners are to decide which solution to suggest to solve the problem.
Teaching style	First-hand experiential
Techniques	1 Teacher organises learners into small groups of three, four or five.
	2 Teacher initiates role play of situation.
	3 Teacher sets up interaction/exchange of views among the learners for group discussion.
Skills	1 Clarity of instruction.
	2 Organisation of learners to participate.
	3 Shaping/guiding behaviour to most efficient end result.

Strategy 2 is much more demanding of a teacher's organisational and educational skills. This strategy requires more planning and preparation, though in class it looks less formal or organised than didactic styles.

If we consider the two strategies and translate them into reality, we can see that the learning is practising totally different sets of skills.

In teaching style 1, didactic/instructional, the pupils are learning how to:
– listen to instructions;
– read a passage carefully;
– give written answers to written questions, ie practise linguistic skills;
– assimilate information which will probably be reference material for a future situation.

In teaching style 2, experiential, the pupils are learning how to:
- listen to instructions;
- work with other people;
- enhance their self-confidence and self-image in a small group situation;
- make real decisions within the simulated situation.

It seems fairly evident from this that, if we are teaching children to understand situations and emotions and trying to increase their awareness of what goes on in human relationships, we ought to make the learning experience as real as possible. If it is real for the children in this practice situation, they are more likely to transfer what they have learnt in class to the real world outside the classroom.

I am not advocating an educational system that is wholly based on first-hand experience. I am indicating that there are different teaching strategies which are appropriate to anticipated outcomes, and which accommodate learning styles, all of which depend on the aims of the lesson as perceived by the teacher. I believe that there are a number of different styles which teachers can build into their professional repertoire, and which they can then select as appropriate to the current task.

B

Basic principles and management skills

The following is a list of the general principles in teaching personal and social education:

1 All teaching is relevant and meaningful to the learner's experience.
2 Knowledge and skills are taught in context.
3 Practice is more important than theory.
4 Maximum pupil participation is aimed for.
5 A good lesson has variety.
6 The teaching goal should be borne in mind.
7 Learning readiness is essential.
8 Learners are informed of what they are doing.
9 All teaching puts the responsibility for learning on the pupil.
10 Positive attitudes are essential.

This list is discussed in detail below, point by point, giving first a brief description of the principle followed by a discussion of specific techniques whereby the teacher can best work towards realising those principles. The advice offered here is not exhaustive, but it is a substantial introduction and teachers will be able to expand their repertoire as they gain practice.

1 All teaching is relevant and meaningful to the learner's experience

Ideas presented to the pupils are of little use unless they mean something to the children who are learning them. Even if those ideas are common knowledge, if the children do not see them as relevant, it is a wasted exercise. For example, nuclear power may be very much in the teacher's mind as necessary for world salvation, but may well mean nothing to the pupils. This is not to say that new ideas should not be presented to the children. Their experience of life is much concerned with new ideas, but those aspects should always be presented in a form which is meaningful and relevant to a learner's experience.

It follows that situations and examples should be couched in terms that the children can understand, and, where possible, in terms that are immediately real to themselves. For example, instead of presenting a story about children in socially deprived areas, the classroom itself could become such an area with a bit of imagination. The story could later act as follow-up/consolidation, but the immediate presentation would have maximum impact on the learners because it came to life for them.

Personal involvement through content

Whatever media or resources are used should focus on the child, rather than some third party, although there are times when third party exercises are essential (see below 'Stories').

I shall mention three examples to demonstrate this principle: the resources of questionnaires, stories and ostensive media.

Questionnaires

These should always be relevant to the pupil. For example:

On friendship
1 What do you think makes a good friend? ....
2 Are you a good friend? ....
3 Is it ever difficult to be a good friend? ....

Self-assessment on studies
1 What is your best subject? ....
2 What is your weakest subject? ....
3 How do you think you could improve in
  your weaker subjects? ....

On personality
Give yourself a score out of 10 on these aspects:
Appearance
Speech
Confidence
Friendliness

On lifestyle

	never	seldom	some-times	often	very often
1 I go to discos					
2 I help around the house					
3 I play sport					

On sociability
1 I am easy to get on with   3 2 1 1 2 3
2 I like other people   3 2 1 1 2 3
3 I have a good sense of fun   3 2 1 1 2 3

There are many types of questionnaires or answer sheets. It is easy to make them up, and teachers can experiment with styles of answers; whether it is a straightforward answer, or a qualified answer, or whether there is a grading scheme on a 'never – very often' scale, or numerical, 3 2 1 1 2 3, 1 2 3 4 5, and so on; and they can experiment with the contents of the questionnaires. A look at the current literature will provide a tremendous source of ready-made questionnaires and work-sheets, and of ideas for teachers to make their own which they may design with the specific needs of their pupils in mind.

Stories

Any stories which are presented should be meaningful and relevant to the pupils. Pupils should be able to identify with the characters and with the circumstances. Stories can be a most powerful medium in getting across ideas in a non-threatening way, and teachers should use them frequently for this purpose.

One of the most powerful elements of stories is that they de-personalise the situation. If the subject matter is in any way threatening, if it is going to introduce an atmosphere of unease or hostility, then a third party ought to be sought.

For example, if the subject matter is the dangers of glue-sniffing, better that the message be contextualised into the form of a story. Or if the subject matter is drinking, or violence, or any turbulent attitudes or actions, it is best to imagine actors rather than encourage the children to put themselves into a first-hand experience of the situation. In this way the pupils will be able to see for themselves the relevance of the message, but they will not be directly practising the situation with its possible harmful consequences. Role play of disturbing elements is to be approached with caution. It is best to de-personalise such aspects so that pupils may see the relevance to themselves, through being able to identify with the characters and decide on courses of action, but not have to practise such behaviours themselves.

Stories may of course be used in a powerful sense to demonstrate positive attitudes and models of behaviour to aim for. We can present positive values through stories, again using characters with whom the pupils can identify. We can take the notion further through role play, get the children to illustrate aspects of the story that were particularly significant to themselves, or write it up in diary form, and so on.

Ostensive methods

An ostensive, observable content is perhaps the most powerful of all the media for building and communicating attitudes, skills and knowledge. The degree of reality will of course be at the teacher's discretion. It can range through simple demonstration, simulation, role play, socio- and psychodrama, to real-life situations.

For example, a pupil can easily demonstrate how to help someone to cross the road, how to organise himself or herself for a homework session, how to ask someone for a dance. Pupils can role play how they would cope with an interview, a tricky situation calling on their honesty, how they would avoid pressures on them to vandalise property. They can actively participate in a real-life situation of welcoming a visitor to school, in going on a field trip, in getting ready for residential or work experience.

Ostensive media and actual engagement are immediately relevant to the children; if they see that the content is going to be about themselves, they quickly join in.

Personal involvement through the process

The first step to success is to get the children to think about what they are doing (content); the second is to get them actually to do it (process).

It is fun to get children to invent their own questionnaires. They will readily respond to this, either by coining their own criteria for the questions, or thinking up the questions themselves. I came across this in a school where children were asked initially to fill in a questionnaire on their own qualities. It first appeared as:

hardworking	lazy
conscientious	slack
regular attender	frequently absent

The children wanted to alter the words into their own terminology. It ended up as:

keen	dead beat
swot	scave
goes to school	bunks

and so on.

To involve the children in a process like this is to get them thinking about and actually defining their own criteria. Once they have consciously identified aspects of life, frameworks, which are important to themselves, we as teachers can help them come to terms with their own place within their framework.

It takes more energy and initiative to involve the children in the process whenever possible. For example, in role play sessions the children themselves may be invited to direct the proceedings, to imagine alternative behaviours and outcomes.

Video is today relatively easily accessible. It is a powerful medium for modifying behaviour or setting 'model' behaviours. Children can see themselves as others see them, and can accept, reject or modify their own behaviour accordingly. They can also move by degrees to a 'model' behaviour, and can watch the outcomes immediately. Just as powerful as the film itself is the process of filming. When I first tried using video as a teaching medium, I was taught how to use the equipment by the children, a group of near-delinquent reluctant 15-year-old learners. Their knowledge of the equipment was impressive. But what was tremendously rewarding was the degree of enthusiasm that they brought to the task of organising the video equipment and themselves to make a film. It is the group co-operation that develops in the making of a film that is the really valuable educational component, as much as the finished article. In fact, the film was never finished. I considered that unimportant, and the children forgot about it. In the same way as, in a discussion lesson, the important element is the process of talking to each other rather than reaching a consensus of opinion, so the most valuable function of filming was the co-operative spirit that developed among the children.

No matter what the medium, the same principle applies. We should strive to make the content meaningful and relevant to the learners' experience, and we should endeavour to involve the learners themselves in the design process. If the whole action-exercise is real to them, they will enjoy it and demand more. Personal involvement never fails. The children themselves are the best resources for any teacher. If we can involve them in their own education, they will certainly succeed.

2 Knowledge and skills are taught in context

New information and skills are more relevant to the pupils if they are presented in context. If the pupils can practise using this information or skill in specific situations, they are likely to recognise what they have already learnt when new, similar situations arise. For example, the idea of 'honesty' must always be presented in context rather than as an isolated concept, divorced from reality. It may be contained in a story, in an exercise, in a dramatised situation, in a pictorial context, in a discussion. The point is that it provides a focus of *experience*. The learners must see the relevance of the concept 'honesty' within that particular context, and find out how they might react themselves. Having encountered this notion in the experimental environment of the classroom, children can then recognise similar situations in real life and be that much more able to cope through the practice and training they have received in class.

This principle also applies to the teaching of specific knowledge. For example, say the children are learning how to open a bank account and are practising filling in forms. It makes sense to have real forms, and to undertake this exercise to encourage the children really to open an account, even in the school bank, if one exists. The exercise could easily expand to a simulation of a bank situation, and other experiences which will assist the pupils' learning. And local managers are usually ready to help when they are invited to do so.

A schematic representation will expand this notion:

Verbal exchanges
  – written reports, situations and stories
  – spoken reports and explained situations
Mediated experiences
  – pictorial situations
  – dramatised situations
  – simulated experiences, including role play
  – videoed and filmed contexts
Real experiences
  – visitors to the classroom
  – field trips
  – residential experience
  – work experience

It is left to the discretion of the individual teacher how near he or she wishes to approximate to reality to get the message across. It is suggested that a rough guide would be: the more abstract the message, the more formal the presentation. The more personalised the message, the more real-life the presentation. To expand this notion:

If the content of the lesson is knowledge-based, for example,
- requirements for entry to different jobs,
- how to use the telephone directory,
- budgeting for a week's living,
formal, written materials are adequate,
- fact sheet,
- the directory itself,
- a budget sheet.
If the content of the lesson is attitudes-based, for example,
- whether to be honest,
- whether to marry someone of a different race,
- whether to continue smoking,

the presentation should be couched in real terms. That reality may be modified if the subject matter appears over-controversial or threatening by de-personalising the situation through stories or role play or film, but the situation should still have immediate impact on the learner. Through this first-hand experience of the situation pupils can see the situation in its entirety and draw their own conclusions.

3 Practice is more important than theory

Teachers are usually only too well aware of this from their own professional experience. It is very useful for us all to benefit from the theoretical foundation that we receive from our institute of education, and also from our continuing in-service education. Yet no amount of theory was as valuable as the on-the-spot training we received at the hands of the children. Indeed, through our class practice we can develop our own theories of education.

That principle is true also for the children, in most subject areas, but particularly in behavioural and attitudinal areas of the curriculum. Through the practice of the exercise, children will experience for themselves what it is all about, and draw their own conclusions, that is, abstract from the whole experience their own theory of life. Through direct, first-hand experience of a concrete situation, children will become familiar with the concepts that we, their teachers, are presenting before them. In this way we are using the classroom as a training ground, as a representation of what the children may expect when they leave it. This familiarity with and realisation of their expectations is much more powerful as an educational exercise than letting the children develop false expectations, and can avoid a lot of confusion and heartache.

The most important thing is to bring the world outside into our classroom through visitors and real experiences, or represent the world through simulation and dramatisation; and, having done this, to let the children experiment and practise within that controlled, supportive situation. This practice is much more powerful than telling. Children will do where they will not listen.

We must ensure the right environment and adequate opportunity for practice. This can be done by following a fairly simple step-by-step procedure of:

- presentation,
- further practice with or without transfer,
- consolidation,
- further practice, usually with transfer,
- revision,
- further practice,

and so on. This sequence of expanding expertise may be applied to most classroom situations where a process of systematic practice is required.

For example, below is a transcription from an actual filmed teaching situation. Our aim was to look at the topic of 'friendship' and discuss the point that sometimes it is difficult to maintain friendships without some friction in relationships, particularly when more than two people are involved. A discussion in threes is in process about 'What makes a good friend'. The teacher wants to introduce the idea that sometimes relationships become strained, and how we can cope with the stress and the threat to the friendship, and how we can resolve the situation.

The teacher breaks into the class discussion.

Teacher: I wonder if three people could help me here? *(Three pupils volunteer.)* Thank you. Now, please tell me your names. *(The teacher did not know the class as we were making the video film for demonstration purposes.)*

Pupil: Kate.

Pupil: Sue.

Pupil: Mandy.

Teacher: Good. Now, let's sort out who's who. *(Arranging girls with Kate in the middle.)* Kate, you are good friends with Sue. Right? *(They agree.)* And Mandy, you and Kate are good friends as well. Right? *(They all agree.)* But Sue and Mandy don't know each other very well. *(Girls laugh.)* Now, Mandy, you and I will go over here for a moment. Kate, you and Sue have arranged to go out tonight and to meet at seven. Would you like to talk about your arrangements? *(Teacher turns away with Mandy. Sue and Kate start talking about this evening.)*

Sue: Let's go to that new disco in town.

Kate: Yes, all right. Shall I come round to your house? *(Meanwhile Teacher and Mandy start talking quietly to each other.)*

Teacher: Now, Mandy, last week you and Kate arranged to go to the pictures tonight, and you're meeting at seven. Go over to Kate and start making arrangements. *(Mandy agrees, goes over to Kate and Sue, and addresses Kate.)*

Mandy: Hiya, Kate, we're going to the pictures tonight, aren't we? *(Embarrassed silence.)*

Sue: No, she's going with me. We're going to the disco.

Mandy: But she's going with me. Kate, don't you remember we arranged to go last week?

Kate: Oh, yes, I forgot. *(Genuinely perplexed, doesn't know how to handle the situation. Pauses, looks from one to the other. Mandy and Sue begin to argue and push each other.)*

Sue: We're going to the disco, so shove off.

Mandy: No, we're going to the pictures. She's my friend, not yours.

Teacher: Stop! Now, let's look at what's happening here. Kate, how do you feel?

Kate: Awful!

Teacher: What are you going to do?

Kate: I don't know.

Teacher: *(to Mandy and Sue, also including whole class.)* What can Kate do now?

Mandy: She could say we could all go together.

Sue: Yes, but you and I don't know each other.

Pupil in class, Penny: She could introduce you to each other and all go together.

Teacher: That's an idea. Could you show us how to do that? Would you like to change places with Kate for a moment? *(Penny stands in Kate's place. Kate stands to one side and watches.)*

Penny: Sue, this is Mandy. Mandy, I'm awfully sorry, I forgot we'd made arrangements to go out. Would you like to come to the disco with us?

Teacher: Mandy, how do you feel?

Mandy: All right.

Pupil in class, Julie: What happens if Sue doesn't want Mandy to go?

Teacher: I don't know. Shall we try that one out? Would you like to take Sue's place for a minute? *(Julie joins in. Sue steps out.)*

Julie: No, I don't want her to come. We're going to the disco on our own.

Kate: That's awful. I'd drop her and go with Mandy.

Teacher: Let's think about this one. Think of another situation like this, where you find yourself in a situation where there is possible conflict between you and friends, where it might be difficult to keep friends.

Pupil in class: If they put you in that situation they're not real friends anyway.

Teacher: That's a very good point. Let's think about that one as well. Now, in threes, could we think up another situation, please? *(The children go back to their discussion groups of threes and talk for a few minutes, without any monitoring by the teacher.)*

Now, may we see some of the situations, please?

The children volunteer to show their own situations. They take it in turns to show them to the whole class. The situations include:

1 Friend A copies homework from friend B and tells teacher it is his own work. Friend C knows. Does he tell?
2 Friend A forgets B's birthday. Friend C gives B a present. B thanks C in front of A. A is hurt.
3 Friend A invites friend B to a party, but does not invite friend C. A meets C and asks her what she is going to wear to the party.

We finished the session here. In all it took about 40 minutes, to show the initial presentation, and then to follow up through the further practice situations.

The methodology here followed the procedure:

Initial presentation through role play. The children experienced the situation for themselves, and thought about means of solving the problem.

Further practice with transfer. This was when the first alternative behaviours were suggested and tried out.

Consolidation. This is where the children thought up their own situations, using the skills that they had learnt, and putting into practice the attitudes of care and willingness to avoid hurt.

In a later session during the month we returned to this theme. The children were pleased to go through their practice situations again. We then expanded the situations into more complex ones, involving the same skills and attitudes, but more related to relationships in general, rather than only to child friends.

For example:

1 Your son/daughter wants to go to a party, but your husband/wife does not agree. What do you do?
2 A colleague at work has had an argument with your boss and tried to enlist your sympathy. You agree with your boss, but you do not want to hurt your friend. What do you do?
3 Your mother insists that the cashier in the supermarket has short-changed her. You think that the cashier is correct, but you do not want to embarrass your mother in public. What do you do?

It is through constant practice that children learn to feel at ease in handling this sort of tricky social situation and feel competent to employ the skills they are learning.

The cycle of presentation–practice–consolidation–practice–revision is applicable to all media, not only that of a dramatised approach. If the subject matter requires verbal or written statements, a similar cycle may be put into action of, say:

- presentation story,
- follow-up through worksheets, giving written answers on the story,
- further reading as practice,
- discussion of further reading,
- original writing, to use and transfer knowledge and skills,

or a multi-media approach of:

- pictorial presentation of a situation,
- written questions to stimulate discussion as further practice,
- discussion,
- written answers as consolidation,
- dramatisation of new situations for transfer, consolidation, revision.

It is worth noting that a pupil can practise a concept right through his school life (see the discussion of Button, 1981, and his table p. 20). Teachers can follow this schema, but amend the topics to suit their own requirements. It is very useful to do this and earmark times during the pupils' school career when they will benefit from a review of what has gone before and further practice, or expanded practice in transfer situations.

One sometimes hears a naïve comment of 'We did "relationships" in the first year' or 'We did sex education in the second year'. This attitude presupposes that once we have 'done' an aspect of personal and social education it is learnt, finished and stored away in the archives. Nothing could be further from the truth. Personal and social education is dynamic; the situations change, though basic principles remain standard. It is up to us, as teachers and supervisors, to arrange for plenty of practice to enable our children to internalise those basic skills and principles in the first place, and to arrange for their use in novel situations.

4 Maximum pupil participation is aimed for

It is important to involve all children as much as possible. The children should become responsible for their own learning; but that means all the children and not just the most confident.

The skills and techniques described below will enable us to develop strategies to involve all children; to encourage the shy and awkward; to channel the energies of the more vociferous and to make them responsible for the shyer ones; to involve every child with the others to his maximum capacity. Personal and social education depends for its success on group co-operation. It maintains the integrity of the individual and develops personal, individual qualities, but it is a social, co-operative process in the main.

There are a number of elements to gain maximum pupil interaction and participation, and many have already been touched on in this book; but for the purposes of this section we can identify three as being of prime importance. They are:
  – traffic in the classroom
  – geography of the classroom
  – style of leadership

Traffic in the classroom

Here are some suggestions for the control and flow of traffic.

Interaction patterns may be one-direction or multi-directional
a)

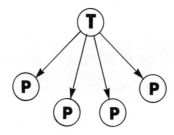

This pattern is familiar in an information-giving session, or lecture. The teacher talks to the pupils who receive the information, and invites neither comments nor questions.

b)

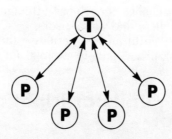

This is a variation on pattern 1, a lecture situation, with the addition that individual pupils are invited to respond to the teacher. It would be basically an information-giving session, with an invitation to the pupils to question the teacher on a point of information. It is probably appropriate to small groups of pupils, where questioning can be kept to manageable proportions.

c)

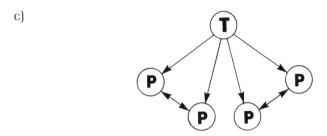

This strategy starts opening up lines of communication between pupils. It is a basic step in establishing group work or total class involvement. The teacher gives the command, 'Ask the person sitting next to you', and then leaves the pupils to do so without any further guidance.

d)

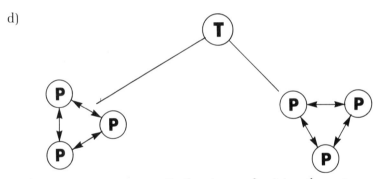

This pattern goes a step further in emphasising the autonomy of the pupils. The teacher's directions are, 'Talk to the people in your group'. Having given them guidance in what to talk about (see next section) the teacher may then get right out of the way and allow the pupils to start talking among themselves.

This strategy is very useful in discussion sessions. It encourages confidence in the pupils. People are usually much more prepared to talk in intimate situations of one-to-one or one-to-a-small-number, particularly if they feel that their opinions will be valued and supported, or at least not aggressively challenged as so often happens in larger gatherings.

A point to note in this strategy is that the teacher should be prepared to be unobtrusive. It is not necessary for the discussion to go via him or her. Pupils can, through this method, find the freedom to explore their own feelings without the veto of their teacher.

e)

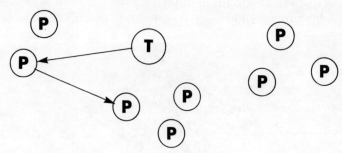

This pattern is useful for opening up class discussion. The teacher invites one pupil to talk to another, probably in another part of the room. This sort of 'expansive' traffic is appropriate to plenary phases of the lesson, when the teacher wants people to listen to each other and exchange information on a whole class basis.

It is a good idea for the teacher to vary his or her position as well. He or she may sometimes move to another part of the room, so as to draw the focus of attention to other people in the vicinity. Always with an eye to variety, the alert teacher could move to groups that are quiet, troublesome, have a lot to say, or become significant in other ways.

Geography of the classroom

Seating arrangements in the classroom may vary from ranked,

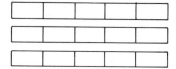

to open plan.

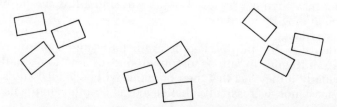

Ranked seating arrangements are appropriate for situations where contact is to be minimised. With this arrangement there is little eye-contact among pupils and restricted physical movement. It is probably the easiest arrangement for unilateral control by the teacher. Its use is appropriate to formal tests or examinations. Because of its geography, it is inappropriate to any form of discussion which calls for personal contact or empathic relationships.

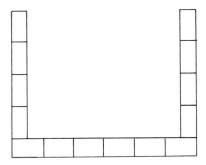

Horseshoe arrangements are appropriate for situations where communication between pupils is encouraged, but still controlled by the teacher. In fact, the teacher would probably have to stay at the desk in this sort of situation. It would be inadvisable for the teacher to attempt to move around, and would certainly be distracting to pupils in the immediate vicinity. This arrangement is appropriate to information-giving sessions where some participation is expected. The teacher can establish a much warmer relationship with pupils if he or she can maintain eye-contact with them, and encourage them to look at each other as well. He or she can arrange for two-way conversations between neighbours – 'Ask the person sitting beside you' – or can arrange for cross-room communication – 'Ask him over here'. The teacher is restricted in setting up any sort of group work, simply because the desks or tables get in the way.

Grouped seating arrangements encourage warm, empathic relationships. Pupils sit in small, intimate groups, facing each other, able to converse within a supportive, non-threatening atmosphere, and free from interference from outside agencies such as the teacher or other groups. In this arrangement it is necessary for the teacher to have an eye to the size of the group, and the relationships among different types of personalities that might be set up.

Groups of three tend to work well in involving all the members (see Button's 'Socratic discussion groups', 1974). Groups of four are in danger of becoming two pairs unless the teacher gives specific instructions for conversations that will include all members: for example, one person is to report to the other three. Five is a useful number, since splinter groups tend not to form from odd numbers; it is more tempting to split a group of four into pairs rather than group of five into a two and a three. Six is about the maximum size for a small discussion group.

With a seating arrangement of small groups the teacher is able to lend words of encouragement, or a supportive presence and is also able to withdraw entirely from an active management in the session, in order to watch the proceedings.

Style of leadership

Style of leadership will inevitably be in accordance with how teachers see their own role. Their style will be reflected in all sorts of conditions in the classroom, including the geographical layout.

Button (1974) has developed a model to categorise styles of leadership. I interpret his model as having a first parameter from 'authoritarian' to 'democratic'. We then imagine a progression from a style of leadership that insists on control to one that encourages participation and mutually-agreed self-government.

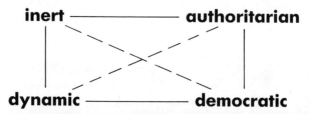

Another arm of the matrix I see as pointing to a progression from 'inert' to 'dynamic'. (I should stress that the word 'inert' does not imply laziness. Some people strive most energetically to be inert. Take, for example, the politician who wishes to maintain the status quo; the mother who wants her children never to leave her and maintains an attitude of benign dominance; the manager who refuses, by a policy of ignoring issues, to accept any sort of change.) A style of leadership that is inert will be immutable. A style of leadership that is dynamic will be interested in promoting the well-being and progress of its personnel.

Inert-authoritarian: the role adopted here would probably be that of a 'disciplinarian' in the traditional sense. Such teachers would probably view themselves as having unilateral control over their class, expect total obedience, and not allow any independence to the pupils in deciding their own destiny. They would be intolerant of change, and probably would not see the need for it.

Dynamic-authoritarian: this leader would dictate change to pupils and insist that they follow in fulfilling his or her perceived needs for them. There would probably be no democratic discussion of needs.

Inert-democratic: a democratic style of leadership will by definition encourage participation on the part of the pupils. However, democracy is ineffective unless guidance is also provided in how to use it. It is no use telling pupils to sort things out for themselves unless clear strategies are presented for their use, or they already possess the decision-making skills appropriate to this sort of situation, and those skills usually develop through appropriate training in making decisions.

Dynamic-democratic: this style of leadership calls for energetic awareness, a determination to involve pupils in their own self-management. A teacher who opts for this style will set up situations, provide pupils with the necessary skills for coping with and successfully resolving those situations, and offer support to the students while they see the task through for themselves.

In terms of planning and implementing classroom actions, this is probably the most demanding of leadership styles, yet certainly the most rewarding in terms of increased personal and social competence.

It seems sensible to suggest, from our understanding of personal and social education, that the implications for a style of leadership are self-evident. The notions inherent in personal and social education of democracy, a child-centred approach to the exercise, a gradual evolution of self-awareness and self-direction, all call for a style from the teacher of energetic dynamic guidance, not of a dictatorial kind, but of a caring, democratic variety.

I know that many colleagues shy away from this notion, since they feel that that sort of participative activity is suitable only for liberal-minded youngsters, new to the profession, with an interest in sociology. This is simply not true. Personal and social education calls for a firm control, a kindly but forceful leadership, a mature wisdom to help but not dictate.

The elements I have outlined of traffic, geography and style of leadership all have a bearing on the amount of pupil participation aimed for. In section 2C hints will be given on specific activity-oriented skills that will be useful in teaching for personal and social education.

5 A good lesson has variety

As in any other lesson, sessions of personal and social education need variety of pace, activity, stimulus, and so on. Any session that lasts for 20 minutes and over must have variety of some sort. To continue the same exercise will result in pupils' losing interest, involvement and motivation.

Experienced teachers know all this, but it is worth emphasising here that personal and social education contains no magic formula for success. Its success depends almost exclusively on the teacher's management skills.

We could regard the phases of a session as following a pattern of:
- set
- presentation
- practice
- consolidation
- transfer
- conclusion

Naturally there will be variations on this theme.

In our lesson planning we could look to an identification of the elements which could be varied, and match them against the basic pattern. So we get an overview of:

	Pace	Resources	Activity	Intensity	Pupil involvement
set	slow	OHP	teacher talks	high	pupils listen
presentation	slow	OHP	teacher talks and questions	high	pupils listen and answer
practice	quick	book	pupils talk	high	pupils talk to each other
consolidation	slow	worksheet	pupils write	low	individual work
transfer	quick	drama	pupils direct the activity	high	all pupils are active; acting, directing or commenting
conclusion	slow	OHP	teacher talks	low	pupils listen – attention focused to next lesson in series

The variation will occur, say, on a termly basis as well as a weekly, or daily; on a long-interval as well as a short-interval basis. In practice this could mean that we may plan in advance not only for single lessons but for a series of lessons.

Suggested lesson plans could be:

1 initial agreement
2 presentation of the theme through drama
3 follow-up through discussion
4 consolidation through writing exercises

or 1 initial agreement
2 presentation of the theme through discussion
3 role play of aspects of the theme
4 discussion
5 gathering of opinion

or 1 initial agreement
2 presentation of the theme through problem situation on worksheet
3 discussion of worksheet
4 filling in questionnaire
5 gathering opinion

Our planning diary could run like this:

Week 1: Tuesday   Year 3

Theme	Caring community
Specific topic	Helping the disabled
Objective	To give pupils direct experience of what it is like to be disabled/dependent, and to have the responsibility of caring for others.
Set	Tell pupils what we are going to study over the next three weeks.
Presentation	Trust walk: working in twos, one pupil leads another who pretends to be blind.
Practice	Feedback of what it feels like to be blind; what it feels like to have the responsibility of leading. Changeover so that both partners experience both roles.
Consolidation	Talking in fours. How do blind people cope?
Transfer	Dramatised situations: how handicapped people in general are dependent on others.
Conclusion	How well did we cope in sharing ideas and experience?

Week 1: Friday   Year 3

Theme	Caring community
Specific objective	Helping the disabled
Objective	To give further practice in concept presented on Tuesday and to consolidate skills and attitudes of care and willing help.
Set	A picture of a guide-dog: a quick response from the class as to what they think working with a guide-dog might be like.

Presentation	Story about a guide-dog and her mistress. Details of individual tricks and preferences, e.g. she didn't like going to the vet and would guide her mistress past the vet's door.
Practice	Discussion about how we would get around with the aid of a guide-dog as opposed to a white stick.
Consolidation/Transfer	Writing in diary form our experiences as a blind person.
Conclusion	Sharing of ideas and how well we coped.

We followed this sort of blocked approach in a school where I was working. I arranged a visit from our local guide-dog owner-speaker, Amy Benson, a good friend of mine. As a follow-up to her visit, I also arranged a visit to the Guide-Dogs' Training School in Exeter, where we met the organisers and saw the dogs in action with their trainers.

Our theme was spread over a year, and involved the whole of the second year at some time or another. We arranged it like this:

Term 1 2TF and 2FL

Term 2 2RC and 2ND

Term 3 2KL and 2GD

(The names of our classes took the initials of the form teachers.)

We adopted a rolling programme which was repeated by terms. We had three aspects to our programme:

(i) **Training and work of guide-dogs.** We chose this aspect because we had already established links with Amy Benson and Exeter through my involvement with the school. It is always the case, however, that individual teachers in schools have their own interests and contacts which they may use to provide a starting-point. For example, animal welfare, care of the elderly, *Blue Peter* and similar projects, and so on.

(ii) **Problems of handicapped people and how they cope.** There was more information-giving in this aspect, since we did not have direct access to any handicapped person other than Amy. Some of the fourth years were working with handicapped and elderly people on Project Trident, a three-part scheme of work, leisure and community care. We invited them to come along to our lessons and share their experiences with us. This exercise also served as a training ground for our second years in receiving visitors to their classes, as did, of course, the visit of Amy and, on another occasion, two colleagues of hers, including her employer.

(iii) **Class project on any other aspect.** This part was chosen through consultation between the children and their teacher. They were at liberty to choose any aspect within the total scheme and follow it through in any way.

The three aspects were rotated so that each group of two classes was fully involved in the overall scheme and they were all gaining the same range of experience.

At the same time the whole of the second year was continually engaged in collecting money for a guide-dog through all sorts of fund-raising enterprises. This activity was spread over the year and could be viewed as both an individual class and a year-group activity. For example, one class decided to sell mince pies at Christmas, as well as collecting ring-pulls from drink cans for sale at the local scrap merchants. At the end of the year we purchased a guide-dog. We organised a competition for choosing the dog's name. The children chose 'Honey', the name of my own dog whom I used to take to school in my car. Honey's photograph now has pride of place in the school entrance hall.

With thought and initiative, a large-scale programme like this may be organised without too much difficulty. We like to think that, as a result of our efforts, a blind person received a guide-dog, our children were fully involved in all sorts of aspects of care, and grew in understanding of what it means to be handicapped, as well as having enormous fun through the whole of their second year. They learned to work together, and they learned to work for someone else without reward to themselves. And we as teachers, too, enjoyed working together and getting thoroughly involved with the children.

But this sort of enterprise must be planned, and planning brings us back to the notion of setting the aims of our main schemes, and planning, through a variety of ways and means, for their realisation. Vivid, dynamic experiences can be ours through a variety of means, and it is up to us, the teachers, to ensure that the children get the maximum benefit through our guidance.

6 The teaching goal should be borne in mind

Teaching goals can be defined in terms of:
- teaching for recognition
- teaching for production
- teaching for consolidation.

Teaching for recognition. This would put the pupil in contact with a situation, but only so far as he was aware of the implications. We would not, at this stage, expect him to make any decisions about the situation, or decide on any behaviours. We would perhaps leave the situation open-ended. Our purpose here is to present the situation, acquaint the pupils with some of its aspects, and ensure that they will recognise it later when we present it again and take action on it.

Teaching for production. By this we mean that the pupil can use his knowledge and skills spontaneously and appropriately. In order to teach for this level we would present as many stimuli and situations, and engage in as many exercises as were necessary to ensure this level of expertise among the learners.

Teaching for consolidation. In this case we would re-present aspects that had been thoroughly examined before and which had been taught for production. We would probably take the same aspect but present it through new material or in a different context. In this way we can test that what has been learnt before for production can be used in similar circumstances, and skills and knowledge can be refined and practised.

An awareness of these levels of proficiency can assist the teacher in deciding on his presentation, resources, style, and so on – all the aspects of the lesson that he will consider in achieving his teaching goal.

For example, say for the third year we have decided on an overall scheme for the spring term of:

Themes	First half	Second half
Study skills	Preparation for end-of-term examinations	Continued
Relationships friends	–	–
Relationships with families	Working with our families to help us cope with decisions about options	Planning for third-year parents' evening
Community service	–	–
Personal interests	–	–
Decision-making skills	Preparation for options	Field trips to different professions Visiting speakers

The team of third-year teachers have here identified their main themes for inclusion in the third-year personal and social education programme. These themes may well be different from those chosen by the fourth-year team, or they may be the same, with one or two variations.

The third-year teachers consider that certain areas are of more importance than others at this stage of the child's school career. The pupils must engage in study appropriate to passing important examinations and these will have an effect on family relationships. The family is inevitably involved when children are going through a major phase in their school life, and if the help of the family can be enlisted, if all members of the family can feel that they are involved too, the children will stand a better chance of success than if they see themselves in isolation. The teachers also see decision-making skills as important at this time when the children are coming up for options in the fourth year. Again, the family is involved if at all possible.

Any point that is particularly important may receive full attention at any stage; that is, it may be taught for production. Other aspects within the total scheme may be seen as equally important (relationships with friends, personal interests, and so on) but not qualifying at this time for full attention. Those aspects may take a second place at present. In our practical school world where time and resources are limited and must be used wisely, some elements must fade temporarily into the background while we deal with the most urgent.

This is true right through the child's school career. In the first year, for example, this year-group of teachers has identified these themes as important:

My place in the school	– who's who
	– geography
	– what do I do if . . .?
Study skills	– the importance of homework
Relationships with friends	– getting on with others
Relationships with authority	– getting on with parents
	– getting on with teachers
Caring community	– an awareness of the needs of others
Leisure	– using one's spare time wisely

The teachers have drawn up a scheme for the autumn term and have used the key of 3 2 1 as denoting the amount of importance to be given to any particular aspect: 3 is maximum and 1 is minimum.

	First half					Second half				
Weeks	1	2	3	4	5	6	7	8	9	10	11
My place in school	3	3	3	3	3	3	3	3	2	2	2
Study skills	–	2	2	3	3	3	3	3	3	2	1
Relationships with friends	3	3	3	3	3	2	2	2	2	1	1
Relationships with authority	3	3	3	2	2	2	2	2	1	1	1
Caring community	–	–	–	1	1	1	1	1	1	1	1
Leisure	–	–	–	–	1	1	1	1	1	1	1

This detailed planning is not often carried out on paper by a form teacher. It might be done at a conscious level by the organisers of personal and social education in the school, and it might be done by the year teachers as a body. Most teachers would have an intuitive awareness of what they are doing, and operate on the basis of 'I will pay attention to such-and-such an aspect as we go on. We'll see how we go.'

Nor is it suggested that such detailed planning is carried out to the letter. We must always allow for flexibility and spontaneity. If the need arises, we must always be prepared to abandon any scheme in favour of something more appropriate or which promises to be better or more efficient for our needs. At the same time, however, it is important for teachers to think consciously and rationally about what they are doing. If such a planning scheme as the one illustrated is appropriate for them, they should use it, or invent one more suitable.

It is also very useful for reinforcing the notion that personal and social education is cyclical, that we return again and again to a topic at different stages as necessary.

For example, the theme of health education is recurrent through the years and within the years. It could take the form of:

Year 1: 1 Basic health and hygiene. Importance of washing and cleaning teeth, etc. Importance of being nice to know.

2 Getting on with members of the same sex. Getting on with members of the opposite sex.

Year 2: 1 Our developing bodies. What we can expect.

2 Our changing feelings towards ourselves and others. How to cope with those feelings.

3 The importance of personal hygiene.

Year 3: 1 Our developing bodies and emotions. How to cope with changes in ourselves and others.

2 Our developing awareness of the opposite sex. How to cope.

3 Basic sex education: physical aspects as well as moral. The importance of stable, happy friendships as a foundation to a lasting relationship.

4 The importance of not getting too involved too young. The importance of saying no and not being pressured by peers.

Year 4: 1 Our responsibilities to other people's emotions. Developing relationships. Preparation for steady relationships.

2 Sex education: physical as well as moral. Contraception. Sexually transmitted diseases.

3 Our responsibility to ourselves to lead full, happy lives.

Year 5: 1 Preparing for life after school. Preparing for adulthood, marriage, responsible citizenship, parenthood.

2 Being a parent. Caring for children.

3 Ways and means of developing our own integrity, of living in society, of realising our full potential.

We would select our teaching goal within the total scheme as appropriate to the needs of our learners at any given time. In this way we can ensure full coverage of the major aspects of personal and social education at the right time during the pupil's school career.

7 Learning readiness is essential

In order for a session to succeed, it is necessary for us to engage the pupil's attention and motivation. We must not only prepare the 'set' of the lesson, that is, introduce the subject matter and prepare for its teaching, but also engage the co-operation of the pupil to partake in that lesson.

In order to achieve this readiness, it is important to establish an agreement that we are all going to work together as best we can. By entering into this contractual relationship with the teacher, the pupils undertake to commit themselves to the exercise in hand. Even if they are not prepared to co-operate for more than that session, they agree to work with other people for a short time.

A contract is a firm basis for an active involvement by all parties. How to effect such a contract, ensure that it does not get broken, and action to take if it does get broken, is described below.

To help colleagues who are trying this idea for the first time, I will here give the gist of what I usually say when faced with a new group of pupils in a new school:

'I wonder if you would like to join with me in an experiment? We hope to follow a number of lessons which will help us to find out things about ourselves, make friends more easily, cope better in school. We shall be doing a number of things that perhaps you don't already do in school. We shall be doing some games and exercises, and talking to each other quite a lot, and inviting people into our class so that we can talk to them. It can be very interesting, and I'm sure you will enjoy it. Would you like to have a go?'

This question is usually greeted by nods or expressions of agreement. Groups of very reluctant learners will also usually agree, but with a 'Show us what you can do' attitude.

'Fine. Before we begin, however, I want us to agree to one thing. During our lesson together we have to agree to work together. This means not fooling around, and, if we don't immediately see the point of what we are doing, to give it a try and let the lesson go on. If we can't all agree to co-operate we can't begin. I'm not asking you to work together necessarily outside this lesson. After the bell goes we carry on as normal. But until the bell goes for the end of the lesson, we must agree to work together. All right?'

I usually get an agreement to work together, even by the most reluctant learners.

After this initial verbal agreement the bargain must be sealed. Button (1981) and Baldwin and Wells (1981) insist on hand-taking to seal the bargain. I very much like the idea, but it can have its disadvantages as I shall point out below.

Most children quickly respond to an invitation to take hands, and, indeed, often expand this notion to a personal ritual. I remember a group of 13-year-old boys who developed a slap-hands and boomps-a-daisy routine, which they saw as a sign that their special relationship of working together had begun.

One of the reasons for taking hands is to stress the importance of physical contact. We tend to be a society of isolationists; we spurn the idea of the necessity of touch. Physical contact is necessary and important to us all, particularly in a dependency relationship. And it is this sort of emotional set that hand-taking can engender; it is a two-way trust that is willingly entered into.

Sometimes youngsters are not prepared to take hands. If they are invited to do so they might giggle or show signs of embarrassment.

71

Sometimes they can even show hostility, and it would be counter-productive to insist that they do. In this case, the wise teacher will be happy to solicit a verbal agreement that yes, we are prepared to work together and will do our best to stick to that agreement throughout the lesson.

What happens if some children opt out and are not prepared to make an agreement to work together in the first place? This can happen, and has certainly happened to me and many other colleagues. The main thing is not to be panicked but to keep a common-sense, level-headed approach at all times. Only one individual might comment, 'No, it's a load of rubbish', or two or three might choose not to join in. That is their privilege and the teacher ought not to feel that he or she has to persuade them unduly. One should certainly try to get them to join in, but, if they really don't want to, one should let them opt out and sit out. After all, this is a voluntary exercise. The others have expressed a wish to have a go. The decision to let a pupil opt out will, of course, depend on the total numbers in the group. If it is a small group of, say, five or six, one or two people opting out would be disastrous and the group could not function. With numbers of eight upwards, however, we would still have a functioning unit and could carry on. Often the one or two lone individuals will find themselves on the sidelines of what looks like fun. When they see the others actively engaged they may want to join in.

Whatever the situation, the teacher should attempt to rehabilitate the opt-outs as quickly and as tactfully as possible. It is often a matter of pride with pupils who have rejected that which their peers are willing to accept, and any intervention on the part of the teacher must be delicate and unobtrusive. The situation can usually be resolved by the teacher setting the group an exercise and then going quietly over to the opt-outs and inviting them to join in. They usually do. If not, that is their choice, and we must leave the situation for another day. I had a pupil sit out for two weeks. He finally joined in with a martyred air because we had to make the group up to an even number. In the end he thoroughly enjoyed himself.

The situation will also probably arise that some pupils will break the contract. They will start being silly or getting up to some sort of unacceptable behaviour. In the first instance it is a good idea to have a private word while there is another group activity going on: 'Don't you remember that we made an agreement to work together?' If the behaviour persists, mention it in public; 'By the way, class, I thought John and Michael had agreed to work together like the rest of us?' In an extreme case we could get the attention of the whole class, review our contract and its implication of promises not to be broken, and suggest that the miscreants behave themselves. In the final analysis, we can invite them to sit out.

If, at any stage, a teacher feels that it is not working, he or she should abandon the whole exercise and do something in a more conventional lein. This is very important. Often teachers feel that, once they are committed on a certain path, they must continue it through to its bitter end. This is not so. If it isn't working, it should be shelved for another day.

Similarly, if teachers feel that five or ten minutes is enough, then they should not feel pressured into doing any more. Some groups respond readily; some do not. Sometimes teachers feel that they have to abandon the project for several sessions or even weeks to get rid of unacceptable elements in the pupils' behaviours and attitudes. It is not a mark of failure on the part of the teachers, as they often feel. It is only a sign that the children just are not ready, for whatever the reason, and perhaps the readiness has to develop before we can embark on a scheme of personal and social education in the first place.

A further progression of lesson readiness, going beyond the initial contract, is to develop an atmosphere of trust. This is essential before further activities can be embarked upon. If children are to talk about themselves, and their feelings, they must be assured that they will not be laughed at or betrayed. Teaching for trust is a delicate exercise. It can be done through trust and empathy exercises, activities which are specifically designed to make children aware of each other as needy individuals, and to develop their own responses to care and support.

There are many of these exercises that are fully described in published courses, and further guidance may be found in the next section of this book. It requires skill and tact on the part of teachers to manage the class situation when using these exercises. They must be alert and vigilant, encouraging and rewarding, inviting the co-operation and confidence of the children. Before that, however, it is very important to have established, as a first base, that initial agreement that we are going to work together in this lesson. Colleagues who try out trust exercises for the first time are usually pleasantly surprised to find that they really do work.

It is also a good idea to reinforce the agreement at the beginning of every lesson, until it becomes the accepted norm by the children. It only takes a moment, but that moment for that initial agreement is golden. It acts as an anchor, the agreement to a relationship that gives a framework to what is going to follow. Without it the lesson is weakened it has no foundation. We have not enlisted the willing co-operation of the children, and that is an essential of personal and social education.

8 Learners are informed of what they are doing

Open exchanges are essential to co-operation and mutual understanding. We have to understand what we are doing if we are to do it well and with conviction. This is particularly important for personal and social education. The point of the exercise is that pupils should be able to conceptualise for themselves out of their first-hand experience of a situation. If their teacher can help them to understand what they are doing by drawing their attention to certain aspects, raising to a conscious level what they are doing intuitively, they will learn and understand those aspects more quickly.

This sort of deliberate explanation is important for at least three reasons:

(i) Pupils are used to a class situation which requires them to sit passively and assimilate. They are not, on the whole, used to an active involvement, nor to an open invitation from the teacher to express their own opinions and be listened to.

(ii) Pupils need to see the point of what they are doing. If they are expected to engage in an exercise which is not meaningful, and does not become meaningful as they go along, they will be justified in losing interest and opting out.

(iii) A clear understanding of the exercise will enable pupils to draw their own conclusions rapidly and effectively, and motivate them all the more to put those decisions into operation, that is, they will transfer their learned skills easily and fluently into new similar situations, and cope that much more readily on entry into the world outside school.

If we as teachers can promote this openness in our relationships with pupils, we will set the example for them to follow in their relationships with each other. Misunderstandings and crises can be avoided if we learn to talk to each other.

For example, a 'life space diagram' will invite the children to put

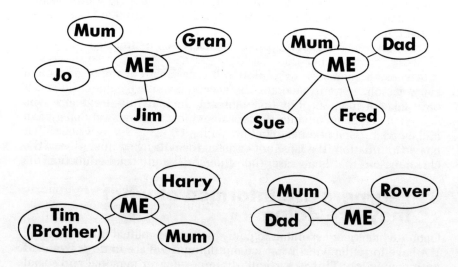

themselves at the centre of the page and then draw in people significant to themselves in relation to their emotional nearness or distance. The physical spaces on the paper will represent the distances in relationships.

Children quickly pick up the rules of the game and perform accordingly. They will also come out with perceptive comments.

'My grandma died last year, but I have still put her on my page because she means more to the family now.'

'My dad left us three months ago. I have put him over the page.'

'I have put my friend nearer me than my brother because he means more. Why is that, that my friend means more than my brother? Is that wrong?'

'My dog is closest of all to me. He is my good friend.'

These are real comments, and they are of a very mature, sincere level. They were made by 12-year-old children of a lower ability range. This is a very important point; we must never underestimate the emotional repertoire of the children, nor their shrewdness in social situations or relationships. Perhaps, sadly, it is a capacity that tends to fade as we grow up; as teachers we should encourage it and keep it alive.

If we tell the children what they are doing and why, this will assist us in two very powerful ways:

(i) **Children will see the point of what they are doing that much more readily, and learn it more efficiently.** I suggested earlier that, if at all possible, we should encourage a problem-solving approach to personal and social education. Such a discovery mission can be fun for the children, motivate them to learn more quickly and more thoroughly, and retain skills and attitudes that they have learnt for themselves much longer than if they had been 'informed'.

Certainly this discovery learning is to be encouraged, and, at the same time, the teacher can help by pointing out certain landmarks as they journey together. For example, if the theme is coping with different cultures and customs, and the specific topic is why some people react hesitantly to cultural diversity, we might take a situation where June takes her German exchange partner to a youth club, or they buy a fish and chip supper and eat it out of the paper. Or we could look at another situation where Bill's Chinese girlfriend invites him to her family's New Year celebrations, and he does not understand the meanings of the dances and rituals.

The teacher might ask the children how they would respond to cultural differences. To help them to articulate their thoughts he or she might write cue words on the blackboard: 'different from' (rather than 'better than'), 'new experience', 'cultures', and so on. The words selected will, of course, be within the conceptual range of the class. By guiding and shaping the children's responses – not telling them what to say, but providing them with the tools with which to express their ideas – the teacher raises the activity, both in its linguistic and cultural sense, to an articulate consciousness.

(ii) **An open atmosphere sets the scene for conduct and relationships.** Children are not generally used to engaging in a collaborative, trusting relationship with their teacher. Perhaps it is so in primary education, where the social and academic structure of the school is quite different from the fragmented hurly-burly of secondary education. The fragmentation of the secondary system and its personnel may sometimes have a divisive influence on the relationships within a building.

To establish such a relationship as the norm can sometimes be a slow and frustrating business, but we have to start somewhere. In personal and social education the responsibility is on teachers to set the scene of an open relationship between themselves and their pupils – not, I hasten to add, a relationship of familiarity and sentimentality which is detrimental to good class practice. Instead it is a warm atmosphere of care which encourages open and challenging exchanges.

If the pupils are encouraged in turn by the teacher to show care and sensitivity towards each other openly, they will not feel embarrassed. If teachers make it their task to encourage warm and empathic relationships, and tell the pupils that they are doing so, the pupils will know what is expected of them. It is sometimes a question of an available model. The children are more used to an image of teachers who are strict disciplinarians and who are not prepared to brook any nonsense. If we can present an alternative model, and make it powerful enough to gain legitimacy in the children's eyes, then we shall have won.

Teaching by example is certainly a very powerful factor in the teacher's repertoire, but that means that a teacher's performance must be as perfect as possible. Teachers have to stand by what they tell the children to do and by what they do themselves. If children are to take teachers as examples and show care and sensitivity to each other, then teachers must show real care and sensitivity to their charges for the children will sense a false presentation at once.

9 All teaching puts the responsibility for learning on the pupil

In personal and social education, the transmission of skills, knowledge and attitudes is not so much a matter of teaching as of learning. As will be seen in section 4A, 'The changing role of the teacher', the actual teaching events in class look more like managing people in social situations than teaching formal aspects of knowledge to a listening audience.

The process of personal and social education, from first to last, is that of an active commitment by the learner to the activity in hand. It is only through active and willing involvement that benefit will be accrued.

If the responsibility for learning rests with the pupil, then the teacher's responsibility is to ensure that he or she engages the learner's readiness, willingness, and active desire to learn. This, of course, is much more complex than instruction, and requires a high degree of skill in social and personal aspects of human exchange. It puts a demand on the teacher's *educational*, rather than *instructional*, skills, and needs patience, tact and good humour.

10 Positive attitudes are essential

Personal and social education is exciting, stimulating, and fun. It is fun both for children and for their teacher. It calls for full involvement, lively presentation, enthusiastic co-operation. It is a participant sport; no one stands on the sidelines here. Children join in readily. Teachers are more wary. They tend to be suspicious for all sorts of reasons that I have already mentioned (see section 1C).

Positive statements. All too seldom in life do people take the opportunity to say something nice, particularly on a personal level. We are accustomed to having criticism levelled against us, and we can cope with aggression. We have learnt the appropriate skills through long practice. Not too many of us cope graciously with positive statements. These are more than compliments which are really designed to flatter. Positive statements say something positive about the person: 'You are a good friend'; 'I am pleased that we have met, for I enjoy your company'; 'You are a good mother to your children'.

One of the most powerful exercises that I have encountered in all the courses and demonstrations of personal and social education that I have seen has been that of positive statements. The principle here is that we take the opportunity to say something positive to each other.

I have seen this exercise carried out, usually at the end of a course, in several different ways. One way has been that each member of the group has a blank piece of paper pinned to his or her back. They circulate, and anyone who wishes may write a positive statement on that piece of paper. If you cannot think of anything positive to say, you don't write anything.

Another way of doing this is for a small group that has been working together to sit in a circle, facing each other, with an empty chair in the middle. Each person takes it in turn to be the recipient of a positive statement. The empty chair is placed facing that one, and each member of the group takes turns in sitting down there, facing the recipient, and makes a positive statement about him or her.

This can be a very moving experience, and one which people carry with them for the rest of their lives. It must be handled with care, for a loose element can be destructive. It can also be one of the most rewarding techniques in a vast repertoire of methodologies, for this exercise is designed to enhance the individual's self-worth and self-esteem.

So many of our children today put a low value on themselves. So many have a poor concept of their own worth. School can really be the place to redress that balance and teach them to value themselves as well as other people. This is not to say that we should teach children to be immodest or conceited. Far from it. Being at peace with oneself and liking oneself is not parallel with conceit. It is an essential element of growing up as a happy, complete person, who is prepared to take his place in society and become a useful citizen.

This positive attitude begins in school. It often does not begin at home, since a lot of our homes can sometimes reflect despair and despondency. It does not begin on television or in any of the other media. It prevails in Church, but Church is sadly unfashionable for most of our youngsters. Where else would they meet positive attitudes but in school?

C

Teaching skills:
specific skills
which are appropriate
to achieving
the basic principles

In the previous section I suggested that there are certain teaching principles which hope to bring out certain qualities in the children. These qualities are significant for the children's personal and social development. This section looks at the teaching principles, and suggests skills, ways and means, which will probably be most useful in realising those principles. They range from simple skills, such as maintaining eye contact with pupils and making sure that they maintain eye contact with each other, to more complex skills such as counselling.

For the purposes of this book it is suggested that there are five major areas which are appropriate. These five 'blocks' incorporate many other skills. The five most widely applicable skill areas would be:

role play	– what it is and how to do it
discussion techniques	– how to arrange for children talking
correction techniques	– how to correct constructively
group work	– how to get group work going successfully in class
empathy exercises	– what they are and how to do them
personal inquiry	– how to get the children to think about themselves and each other.

As in any list, this one is not exhaustive, but it is a good beginning and offers a useful checklist for the teacher in planning a lesson.

Role play

Role play is one of the most powerful techniques at the teacher's command, not only in drama and personal and social education, but in all lessons in the curriculum. It is a shame that it is vastly underused in lessons outside drama, since it has immediate impact and is a tremendous resource for teachers. I would recommend it to colleagues, to give it a try in all their lessons. I feel they will be pleasantly surprised at the simplicity of its management, and the enthusiasm it arouses in the children.

There are a number of books on the subject, the most useful of which are cited in the bibliography (p. 162). For our purposes here we can look at three elements of role play:

1 What it is
2 How we can use it
3 How to do it

1 What it is

It is necessary to remember that there are different degrees of reality in role play. It can range from simple drama, which is an approximation of reality, to a situation which is absolutely real. Whichever level of reality is chosen will depend on what the teacher wants to achieve in that lesson.

Before beginning, please note that it is best to avoid role play in areas of controversy or anything that is liable to offend. For example, say the lesson is trying to get across the concept of honesty. This is a delicate area, since children might feel sometimes that their own honesty is under scrutiny. The wise teacher will look to strategies which make the subject matter meaningful and relevant to the children but not too personalised. It would be unwise here to ask children to role play a dishonest person. The children might feel that the teacher had singled them out deliberately, and they would certainly be practising habits in a real-life situation which would not be in their best interests. In this sort of controversial area, it is best to depersonalise the situation.

For example, the following situation concerns three boys, Harry, Keith and Bob. Keith is friends with Harry, and Keith is also friends with Bob. It is Harry's birthday. He has been given £5 as a present. Keith knows this. Harry leaves the money in his jacket pocket in the changing rooms and goes off to play football. Bob enters, goes through pockets, finds the £5 and takes it. Keith is still lacing his boots. He sees Bob take the money. What does he do?

In this situation, which is probably used in problem solving, we would be unwise to ask the children to take parts in a role play style, that is identifying with characters. The child who was playing Bob would be at risk. The wise teacher would use a pictorial presentation, either drawing it on the blackboard or handing out a worksheet, or give out a script which the children would read for themselves.

It is acceptable to use role play in its different degrees of reality in positive, meaningful situations which highlight areas of behaviour to be aimed for, rather than those to be avoided.

The degrees of reality practised will depend on teaching aims. The degrees of reality can be catalogued as:

abstract	–	familiarity with a situation	–	through reading
			–	through a picture situation
			–	through listening
mediated	–	a represented situation	–	through video
			–	through drama
			–	through discussion
real	–	direct experience of a situation	–	through role play
			–	through arranged real experiences

The following guide-lines are offered to help teachers to determine when they should use any sort of experiential strategy and at which level they should pitch such techniques.

a) Abstract

This is presenting a situation for recognition (see principle 6; teaching goal). It is useful in controversial areas where sensitivities might be threatened, as in the example already mentioned.

b) Mediated

This is represented reality. Teachers may use drama, where children are asked to act out parts, rather than take on a role; or video, where children may see themselves in a part, and either accept or reject that represented behaviour.

This is useful in modelling (see pp. 83, 84) where children are experimenting with alternative behaviours. For example, the children in a group might be asked to take on a different style from their customary one in real life; a shy person might have to act out a person with a dominant streak, or the class clown might be asked to be the responsible leader, or a disruptive pupil might be given a peace-maker's role. The teacher would present the children with a situation, appoint these new roles, and ask them to act out the situation in their new styles.

Sociodrama and psychodrama also appear in this category. 'Sociodrama' is the term applied by Leslie Button (1974) when looking specifically at the role playing of social situations. It helps the children to examine real situations that surround them, and there are many concrete examples of this skill in Button's book.

'Psychodrama' is the name given to a technique developed by Moreno (1964) in the treatment of patients with mental disorders. In this technique the child directs the action of the rest of the group, allocating to them roles of people with whom he or she normally interacts, as well as giving someone the role of him or herself. The child directs the action of a very simple situation in which he or she is involved. He or she lets the actors enact that scene, but indicates to them if they interpret behaviours incorrectly. 'No, my father wouldn't do that', they might say, or, 'No, I would do such-and-such'. This sort of action can have a powerful impact on youngsters in letting them see for themselves how they react in any given situation.

c) **Real**

These are real situations, although they might be contrived, 'set up' in order to achieve certain insights by the children into their own behaviours or to practise certain skills. For example, receiving a visitor is an excellent way of increasing children's social confidence and competence. The exercise calls for a group of children to receive a strange adult. They must arrange between themselves to collect the person on entry to the school, escort him or her to their group, perhaps in their own classroom, engage him or her in conversation for 20 minutes, thank him or her, make their farewells, and escort him or her to the point of departure – all without assistance by their teacher.

The exercise of course needs a lot of preparation and practice, as well as very careful, detailed guidance from the teacher in its planning stages. The planning would include the preparation of an agenda for the conversation, where each member of the group decided in advance which aspect of the conversation he or she would initiate and be responsible for. When the actual visit takes place, the teacher must not help out; he or she has helped the children to prepare, and now it is up to them. He or she should stay in the room, keeping an eye out for any disasters, but should busy him or her self with something else, such as marking books – ostensibly!

This exercise uses role play on at least two levels. First, the children are taking on roles of caring, responsible people who are in charge of a social situation. They are forced to accept these roles to ensure the success of the exercise. Secondly, the exercise itself is a contrived situation, deliberately geared towards eliciting certain kinds of behaviour from the young people; yet it is a real situation.

In fact, what usually happens is that the group gets through the planned agenda for their conversation quite rapidly and the whole situation relaxes into real-life conversation within five to ten minutes. The visitor is also aware that this transformation will take place. Visitors must be chosen with care to ensure that they are aware, sensitive adults who will lead the children on to their best potential.

This is an exercise with built-in transfer from a contrived experience to a real experience. The transfer takes place so rapidly within the exercise as has just been described, that the children will quickly forget that this is a practice situation and turn it into a real encounter. And secondly, the inherent skills and attitudes in this exercise can be immediately applicable to similar situations outside the classroom. It is truly a very useful exercise.

2 **The uses of role play**

Role play is used to make experiences real to a greater or lesser degree.

In doing so it may have, among others, the functions of:
- identifying problems
- solving problems
- avoiding problems

Identifying problems

Very often young people cannot understand why people find fault with them. Even when they do, they find difficulty in pinpointing exactly what they are doing wrong. This is particularly true of non-verbal aspects of behaviour, where gestures and other aspects of body language convey the sense of what the young person is trying to communicate.

Role play lends itself to identifying problem areas through a close scrutiny of all the factors. For example, at a very simple level, a child might wonder why people complain that he or she is surly. A videoed conversation with a friend might show him or her, when he or she watches the film, that he or she should smile more.

At a more complex level, where another child seems to be encountering a lot of criticism from parents for what they call 'unreasonable behaviour', he or she could act through a typical situation involving various members of the family and attempt to identify the problems. The technique of psychodrama (p. 81) may well be useful here.

Solving problems

Once problems have been identified, role play can be used extensively for problem solving in that it is a key to generating new behaviours. Following on, for instance, from the example just quoted of the child looking closely at the behaviour of him or her self and other members of the family, he or she could imagine a solution to the problem just identified. If, for example, the child feels that he or she is, as the parents maintain, being unreasonable in one aspect or another of his or her behaviour, he or she can try out a different way of behaving within the role play situation. In this particular instance, the child and the class are looking at a typical family situation. They are acting it out. The individual child, or perhaps the whole group, have seen where the problem lies, and now have to do something about it. They could suggest new ways in which they might remedy the situation. Perhaps the child could direct the person playing him or her to behave in a different way; or perhaps the group might ask him or her to consider acting in a different way.

Another aspect to be considered in generating new behaviours is that of modelling. This exercise looks at 'ideal' behaviours that are to be aimed for. For example, if a fifth-year group is preparing for interviews with prospective employers, they could practise interview sessions with each other and decide for themselves who would stand most chance of getting the job and why. They could decide on which aspects are most important – a courteous tone of voice, answers which show a responsible attidude, and appropriate appearance. Video can be particularly useful in this sort of exercise, but it is not essential. Group discussion can highlight aspects which the group itself has identified as important.

If the group or any individual is unsure as to what are other people's expectations, they could watch a 'model' behaviour. This would be a demonstration by someone who had 'got it right', who could put on a performance that everyone would agree to be ideally appropriate to that particular situation. The children may watch and then try it out for themselves. Each child's performance could be monitored by the rest of the group, and they could make suggestions for modification or improvement. 'Smile more; don't say that; look more interested', and so on. This 'shaping' or progressive focusing on aspects of behaviour will let each child at least see what is expected of them, and allow them to practise and work towards a standard that is approved by the group, and within the supportive framework of that group.

Avoiding problems

This is a progression from the previous two steps, of identifying problems and of solving problems. This aspect looks at how children may be shown how to avoid problems in the first place.

In very similar ways as have already been described, groups may look at areas of experienced or possible conflict. For example, confrontations with parents are usually familiar to youngsters. We could take a situation of, say, someone coming home later than the agreed time to find their parents fuming as they wait up. A row quickly develops and tears follow.

A role play of this situation could show (1) why the row develops and (2) how it could have been avoided by better management of the situation. The group can practise the roles of offending child and of offended parents in turn, experiencing for themselves what it feels like to be in that situation. Through practising and trying out the experience for themselves they can see better how to avoid conflict in the first place.

Again the value lies in the nature of the practice undertaken in class. Here is an opportunity for the children to try out coping with a situation with all its inherent difficulties without fear of having to pay the price for those difficulties. They can experiment; they can develop insights and awarenesses which are, sadly, usually learnt through real-life experiences and which often leave scars. Role play takes the danger away.

3   How to do it

In my opinion, the best discussion of role play in action is to be found in a little handbook by Roger Lewis and John Mee. (For further reading see bibliography p. 162.)

The authors indicate four stages of role play in action: before you begin, starting, controlling it, and ending it, and they give advice for each stage.

In setting up and controlling role play there are certain fundamental issues to be borne in mind, and these include:
– appropriate attitudes are essential;
– the teacher should be manager but not director.

Appropriate attitudes are essential

Role play should be conducted in a collaborative spirit. It is essential that teachers do not give the impression that they already know the answer. It will be destructive of the group spirit if they feel that they are acting as guinea pigs for an omniscient controller.

The teacher should be the manager, not the director

There is of course a sharp distinction between these two functions. A manager arranges things so that the participants can explore their own feelings and reactions; a director will dictate what the outcomes should be. Role play is for the participants to experience. With this in mind, the skilled teacher will adopt a managerial role, helping them to plan, making suggestions as to how they should conduct the exercise, hinting at behaviours they might care to look at. It is a highly skilled process and not learnt overnight.

When they encourage experiential exercises such as role play, teachers are encouraging the group to decide for itself. They will naturally point out possible difficulties or danger areas, but they will not insist on pupils behaving in a certain way if they so desire. Wise parents will let their children find out by their own mistakes, but try to avoid those mistakes being too painful. Wise teachers will do the same.

Once the action is under way, teachers step aside. They do not need to pass judgement or be the centre of attention. The limelight is for the children. This does not mean that the teachers now abdicate responsibility. Rather they undertake a watching brief, and, if they feel that a valuable point is going unnoticed, they will arrange for its inclusion in the lesson. They might politely interrupt the action, for example, (see pp. 54, 55, 56) and put forward a point of view for the group's attention. They might feed in a cue word. They might suggest that another person takes over a role within the action.

Using the three elements of role play, therefore, lesson plans can be plotted in terms of (a) the degree of reality we wish to achieve; (b) the chosen function of role play as it applies to present purposes in this lesson; (c) the style of presentation that we shall adopt. All these aspects are interdependent, and the choice of one will affect the choice of another.

Discussion techniques

As with role play there are a number of books which look at the techniques of discussion. I recommend Hopson and Scally (1981) as a good checklist against which teachers may plan their lessons.

We need to be aware of certain fundamentals of discussion in personal and social education. These fundamentals would include:
1 different types of discussion
2 how to get the discussion going
3 how to make the children do the talking
4 correction techniques

1 Different types of discussion

'Discussion' is a generic term that most teachers use when they refer to a talking activity by the children. In fact, there is probably not so much real discussion among children as small areas of chat. This in itself can be very useful, since most children find extended talking time difficult to sustain (as do many adults) and can cope only with small amounts of talk. For that talk to be most useful it needs to be structured. Idle chat is wasteful of time and energy – structured chat can be invaluable.

The types of talk most commonly used in class may be listed as:

Paired talk: This is between two people, of course, and is very useful to start discussions among larger groups, as a means of quick opinion gathering, or to break up activities and phases of the lesson.

Talk in threes: This is what Button terms 'Socratic group discussion'. Three is a very useful number of people, since the third person often provides a balance. Opinions tend to be more democratically shared between three people than between two.

Buzz groups: These groups may number from three to ten. The group is given the task to talk quickly among themselves, to gather opinion rapidly, either as a whole group or in smaller sub-groups. It is a useful device for breaking up activities or phases of a lesson. The teacher simply gives the instruction, 'Talk to the person(s) sitting next to you'. Buzz groups may or may not have an appointed leader.

Brainstorming: This is a well-known exercise for eliciting information and ideas from a group of people. The group should be kept to no more than 15, otherwise it might get unwieldy. It is possible to operate with larger groups of up to 30, but the danger here is that not everyone will get a chance, and the shyer ones will probably remain silent.

The group is asked to offer any ideas they have about a particular subject. They call out the ideas and the teacher or recorder writes the ideas up, usually in a shorthand form, on the blackboard or a flip chart. No ideas are rejected or censored at this stage, and the group is invited to react spontaneously and enthusiastically. What is recorded is then used as stimulus for further discussion among the group or as specific input by the teacher. He might ask the group to analyse the information offered, or he might use it in its raw form.

Brainstorming is deliberately unstructured. It is the teacher's task to shape some sort of structure out of it.

Group discussions: For a useful discussion to develop, the group should be kept to no more than eight, otherwise individuals will feel inhibited and reluctant to share opinions. A warm, intimate atmosphere can be encouraged with groups of three to eight.

It is vital that guidance should be given for specific discussion. If the group is told to 'talk about it' they will not know what sort of points they ought to be focusing on, or who is the leader of the group. People need to be guided and helped in talking time as much as in any other social activity.

First the teacher needs to provide an agenda. This is crucial. It is pointless to tell people to talk about something in a vacuum. The concept of an agenda is very important, but very simple to put into practice. It is simply that the teacher offers three or four points for the group to focus on, to start them off.

For example, say the topic is about studying. The teacher could give the pointers to the class:

In your discussion, talk about the following three points:

1 What makes a good student?

2 Am I a good student?

3 Do I need to improve in any way?

Or the topic could be about starting work and appropriate attitudes. the teacher could say:

Talk first about these points: Which is more important – good timekeeping, a smart appearance, or being a quick learner? Or are they all equally important?

At this stage of guidance it is useful to couch questions or points for discussion in closed rather than open terms; for example:

– Which is your best subject at school?

– What qualities do girls look for most in boyfriends?

– Why should we do our homework first before watching TV?

rather than:

– Talk about your subjects at school.

– Which boys do girls like?

– Do you watch TV first or do your homework?

The teacher must be aware constantly that the guidance and structure come from him. Having provided it, he should then let the groups talk among themselves without any monitoring until it is time to call them back together again.

Secondly, the teacher should always appoint a leader or ask the members of the group themselves to select somebody. It is usually more diplomatic to ask for a 'spokesman' or 'spokeswoman' rather than a 'leader', which might carry authoritarian overtones.

It is useful to give the group a task or objective to their discussion and to ask them to report back, through their spokesman or woman, at the end of the talking session. This will make them focus on specific points, and will also make them get on with the job of talking. Groups often waste time talking about what they should be talking about, rather than talking about the specific topic. The simple instruction of 'Talk about this for five minutes. Please report back to the class at the end.' will ensure a quick focusing on the topic, and a speedy gelling of the group.

2 How to get a discussion going

This is such a simple technique that it is surprising it is not used more in oral lessons. It is called 'Snowballing' and it goes like this:

(i) Teacher presents the topic.
     Gives a specific presentation, and hands out a worksheet. Talks for five minutes. Wants to get a quick involvement by all members of the class. They number 25, and they are sitting in individual chair-desks around the room.
(ii) Teacher says; 'Draw your chair up to the person sitting nearest you and ask him or her these questions:
     1 Do you agree with what the teacher says?
     2 If not, where do you disagree?
     3 What would you say instead?
     Person A asks Person B, and then we change over so that Person B asks Person A.'
     Having given this guidance, teacher withdraws from the action.
(iii)The two people do as requested and are usually soon engaged in lively conversation. This is where the teacher must keep a watchful eye. If there are two people who are obviously not getting on, or finding it difficult to talk to each other, the teacher should go to them and help to get their conversation going. He or she can simply say to Person A, 'Ask B to tell you what he thinks,' and smilingly encourage them to talk together.
(iv) The teacher should judge the timing of this phase carefully. It could last up to five minutes. When the teacher feels that it has peaked, and does not want to lose the momentum, he or she will move into the next phase of pairing up the twos. This is done by saying: 'Each pair please draw your chairs up to the nearest pair and form a four.' The teacher monitors the action. If there is an odd pair over a group of six can be made. The teacher then gives the next bit of guidance, probably in the form of another agenda. The simplest way is to start off on familiar territory with what each pair has already discussed. The teacher might say, 'Will each pair tell the other pair what they have discussed and decided. When you have done that, please then consider these points . . .' and would go on to give two or three more points for them to talk about. The teacher then retires but

keeps watch for any four that might not get on too well. If the teacher sees this, he or she quickly goes to guide the conversation on.

(v) This phase should last about five to eight minutes, and the teacher must be sensitive to the total 'feel' of the session. If he or she wishes, the groups of four may join into groups of eight, when they will form larger discussion groups. This should now be the end of the chain, as any more than eight will put an end to informal, empathic talk.

Snowballing can be used in a variety of situations. It is very useful for getting strangers to talk to each other, and it can be used with very large numbers. I once spoke to a gathering of about 150. I felt that I needed to get some audience participation, so said, 'Turn to the person sitting beside you and ask him or her the following questions:

– What has she been talking about?

– Do you agree?

– What do you think of it so far?'

This was only the first stage of snowballing, and I could carry the activity no further, since the audience were sitting in a lecture hall with fixed seats; but on other occasions where they have been sitting on free-standing chairs, I have set up twos leading to fours, and this with audiences of 100 to 150.

This sort of involvement of the audience or class also takes the pressure off the teacher for a short while, and gives a breathing space to gather thoughts and energies. It can be used frequently in a total session, perhaps two or three times in a 45-minute session. The audience or class enjoy it, and feel involved. It is a valuable technique, sadly underused, which ought to be more in evidence in our schools.

3 How to make the children do the talking

It is very easy for teachers to fall into the trap of thinking that ours is the ultimate opinion. As I have said at other points in this book, a consensus is not always the real aim of a lesson. The main aim is probably to get the children talking and listening to each other with respect and sensitivity.

It is, however, sometimes difficult to make the children do the talking. They might be shy, or not know what to say, or expect the teacher to give them the answers. Our aim in personal and social education is to encourage them to find their own answers by exploring their own thoughts and reactions and testing them against the thoughts and reactions of others.

Some obvious techniques here would be:

a) Give guidance through an agenda.

b) Try to deflect a question so that another child answers it.

c) Adopt an attitude that encourages children to feel that their opinions are valued, and more valued than the teacher's.

a) Give guidance through an agenda

I have already outlined the importance of an agenda. It provides a focus, a hook on which to hang conversations. It takes the pressure off the children from grasping at ideas of what to say, and gives an immediate lead into natural conversation.

b) Try to deflect a question so that another child answers it

But not so much that children might feel that you are dodging the issue or have no intelligent answer to give! More of this later.

The idea of deflecting an issue might seem like the skill of the politician. We are told that politicians always answer one question with another. Yet there is real sense in this. It puts the onus back on the questioner. Questions are often asked, not because the questioner does not know the answer, or wants to hear an answer from someone else, but because he or she wants to explore their own ideas, and asking a question is a natural form of expression, using a partner as a sounding board. Teachers are aware of this intuitively, and often avoid giving direct answers to questions quite genuinely because they want the children to do the thinking.

For example, the conversation in this class was about the importance of calling pupils by their first names. The boys objected strongly to being called 'Andrews' or 'Jones'.

'I think it's downright rude of teachers to call us by our surnames,' commented one boy. 'What do you think, Sir?'

'I think I share your opinion,' answered their teacher, 'but what about the rest of us? Have you asked Tom what he thinks?'

The very complex skill of counselling sometimes revolves around this concept. Take this conversation, for example, between a first-year pupil and the year tutor.

'Miss, the other girls in class don't like me.'
'What makes you say that, Sally?'
'They always call me names, and they don't sit by me.'
'Why do you think they do that?'
'I don't know, Miss.'
'Have you had a quarrel with them recently?'
'No, Miss.'
'Have you done anything to upset them?'
'No, Miss.'
'Then why should they behave like that?'
'I don't know, Miss. They just do.'
'Shall we talk to them together?'

'No, Miss.'
'Why not, Sally?'
'Because they'll laugh at me.'
. . . and so on.

This type of conversation goes on many times a day in a secondary school, and wise teachers will try to find out what is at the bottom of the trouble by getting children to analyse the situation themselves. If the children can see what is going wrong, there is a better chance of putting things right than if the teacher wades into action without a clear idea of the background.

Deflecting the question is not always easy, particularly when we feel that our opinion is genuinely being sought. If that is the case, of course, and if the children really want to know what we think, we should give an honest answer. It can be quite infuriating to have people dodge the issue. In class this can take the form of:

'Miss, what do you think of Duran Duran?'
'I'm not sure. What do you?'

Yet this sort of response is useful in personal and social education when we want the children to explore their own ideas.

'Miss, what do you think of mixed marriages?'
More to the point, what do you think?'

The skill of deflecting questions can be quickly learnt. It is important, of course, to judge the time correctly when we should deflect questions. Sometimes there is a clear need for an honest opinion and a straight-forward yes or no, as in:

'Miss, my boyfriend wants me to go all the way. I can't ask my mum. What shall I do?'

'You mustn't, Julie. Just think of what he is asking you to do, and what it means. No, Julie, I don't think that's a good idea at all.'

The social skill of asking and answering questions is as applicable in ordinary class management as in other welfare areas of counselling. This highlights again the fact that the edges blur between what is traditionally viewed as academic classroom activity and active pastoral awareness in our class practice.

c) Adopt an attitude that encourages children to feel that their opinions are valued, and more valued than the teacher's

When all is said and done, it is a personal involvement by the teacher that is the major influence in class. A teacher may put into practice all the techniques and skills that are outlined in this book, yet not be successful in achieving the aims for the children. It is the subtlety of the teacher's role that is crucial. They can make or mar the classroom action by a gesture, a look, a silence. They are the leaders, whether in an active or an inactive mode, and the children look to them for approval.

In section 1B I suggested a theory to explain personal development. This 'competence' refers as much to the teacher as to the pupil. Teachers may be highly skilled at a surface level, but unless they commit themselves to what they are doing, actively put their care into practice, it will not ring true and the children will quickly sense an underlying falsity.

Correction techniques

One of the most obvious ways of encouraging children is to look at ways in which we show our approval. It is easy to approve when the child does something correct. We applaud and offer words of praise, and smile. It is not so easy to encourage when the child is doing something wrong, and that is the focus of this section.

One of the most powerful words in the language is No. Perhaps not enough of us are aware just how often we say it to the children. It can have a really damaging effect, in that it can reduce the status and worth of children in the eyes of themselves and their peers.

For example,
'Miss, may I underline my titles in red, please?'
'No. Use blue or black.'
or:
'Sir, can I borrow a pencil?'
'No. Sit down.'
The art of deflecting questions is useful here:
'Why do you want to use red today instead of blue?'
'You really should have brought one.'

An outright, condemning NO is to be avoided if at all possible, as should any form of correction by the teacher which could be destructive.

For example,
'Don't . . .'
may be rephrased as,
'perhaps you shouldn't . . .'
and,
'I didn't ask you. I asked Sheila'
could be,
'I thought your name was Susan?'
or,
'Shall we listen to Sheila?'
or,
'I think Sheila wants to answer.'

Body language is very important here. It is essential to smile and be encouraging; to make hand gestures that are of an inclusive, embracing nature, rather than to reject; to nod sympathetically and understandingly. It is our job to help the children get over their mistakes and come to an understanding of what is required, rather than to reject them out of hand.

This aspect is probably the most important of all. Teachers must adopt attitudes to the children that they expect the children to adopt to them and others. Courtesy and compassion are as relevant for children as for adults. They are the adults of tomorrow. If they can't learn from us, who is there to teach them? And what will they teach to their children in turn?

It is sometimes very difficult for us to keep this in mind, all the time, but that is what teaching is: showing that we believe in what we are doing and saying. If we are prepared to practise what we preach, perhaps we can then expect the children to do the same.

Group work

There is a good deal of guidance available in the literature on this aspect (Hopson and Scally, 1981; Button, 1981; Stanford, 1977) and I shall not duplicate here the advice offered by these books, but offer a few basic points for teachers to consider in deciding how and when they should introduce group work, and the aspects they need to bear in mind.

1 Size of group

Group work can function successfully, with the teacher still taking an active, personal part, with classes up to 15–20 (see p. 112). If the total group is larger than that, the teacher must delegate the leadership of each sub-group to a pupil. He or she remains the manager of the class session, but cannot maintain personal contact with individual members of the smaller groups.

2 Different types of members in the group

Sometimes teachers might want to allocate specific personality types to a group. They might want to put a shy person in a group with a dominant personality, so that the two would balance each other. Having done that, though, they would certainly structure the activity so that the shy one would not be eclipsed. They might try a role reversal, say, where the shy one had to take on the leadership of the group. They might deliberately structure it so that an aggressive child had to play peace-maker. Hopson and Scally (1981) offer a comprehensive section on dealing with special individual differences in class, and their advice applies equally well in group work.

Often groups will form themselves in already existing friendship patterns. This can sometimes be very useful, particularly in the early stages of group work, when we want the children to feel as comfortable as possible. Later, however, it might be wise to break diplomatically into these patterns, and guide the children on to other partnerships or group dependencies. This is where the teacher sometimes has to take an assertive stance, since children are often reluctant to leave tried and trusted friends and break new ground. The teacher sometimes has to be quite forceful about this. There is nothing wrong, and everything right, in fast friendships, provided they do not exclude the possible formation of new relationships.

3 Uses of groups

There are a number of uses of groups, from opinion gathering and sharing, to peer counselling and peer teaching. Of all the functions, these last two are the most valuable, yet the most time-consuming to put into practice. In this light, the group has taken on learning as its own responsibility, and is now branching out into self-direction so much that it can take on its own teaching.

By 'taking on learning as its own responsibility' I mean that the group now functions well as a unit, always, of course, maintaining the integrity of its individual members. The group is now skilled in talking together and finding answers to its own questions, through discussion, experimenting, role play, and so on. A step further is what I have referred to as 'taking on its own teaching'.

Over a period of time, and with much guided practice, the group will learn how to be independent of the teacher. In the first stages of group work they may still look to the teacher for the answers. He or she will use skill and patience to gently return the responsibility to them, to talk among themselves and discover their own answers.

It is a short progression now to where the children are teaching each other. Instead of taking their questions and problems individually to the teacher, they will learn, with guidance, to take those questions and problems to each other. This can be a very powerful teaching medium, probably the most powerful of all, since the children are accepting a dual responsibility. They are first accepting the responsibility for their own learning, and also accepting the responsibility for helping others to learn; that is, they are teaching. The very process of teaching, as they are now doing, is probably the most efficient way of learning.

Empathy exercises

These exercises really do work. Teachers who have never seen them done, or seen the result of them, are frequently suspicious. The best way for teachers to find out about such exercises is to experience them personally. Most in-service courses in personal and social education will start off with a trust exercise. It is not a teaching device so much as an experience deliberately contrived to get the participants into an appropriate 'set' and to establish an agreed atmosphere of working together and trust.

Below I have described two types of empathy exercise; one physical and one conversational, to illustrate the types of exercise available and to try to explain the philosophy behind the action.

Exercise 1

In this exercise the teacher asks the children to find a partner. If the children already know each other they will gravitate towards existing friends.

The teacher then gives the instructions:

'*In the partnership I would like one of you to be blind for a few minutes – not just pretend to be blind but actually be blind; feel what it's like, think what it's like.*
'*The other person must lead the blind partner for a few paces.*'

This is usually greeted with amusement but general enthusiasm to get on. The teacher cautions the children:

'*Before we start, let's look at how we lead people. Could someone help me a moment?* (Someone always volunteers.) *Now you are blind and I am going to lead you. All right?* (The pupil agrees. The teacher takes the pupil limply by the hand and starts to drag the pupil along. He stops and asks the pupil.) *How do you feel?*'

Pupil: 'Awful!'

Teacher: '*Why?*'

Pupil: 'Because I don't feel safe!'

Teacher: '*Tell me how to hold you. Class, what shall I do here?*'

There usually ensues a discussion as to how one should lead and hold a blind colleague. The teacher now holds the pupil round the waist with the left arm; the right hand is holding the pupil's right wrist.

Teacher: '*Is this more secure? Right? Let's go.*'

They take a few paces.

Teacher: '*How do you feel?*'

Pupil: 'All right.'

Teacher: '*Now, let's all have a go for just a few seconds. Slowly. Right? Off you go.*'

The pairs take only three or four steps before the teacher stops them again.

Teacher: '*Stop! How do you feel, you people who are blind. Are you secure?*'

Various reactions; some yes, some no, some not sure.

Teacher: *'Tell your partner how to hold you if you don't feel sure. Let's have another go. Off you go.'*

The teacher lets that partnership walk half way round the room, then stops them.

Teacher: *'Stop! Blind people, how do you feel?'*

It is at this point that the pupils will offer their own feelings: 'I feel safe'; 'He's pulling me around'; 'I trust her' and so on.

Teacher: *'And the leaders. How do you feel?'*

Again we can expect a variety of reactions. Among them will surely be the following:

'I feel unsure at leading her.'
'It's a big responsibility.'
'I hope he trusts me.'
'I'm scared he'll bump into something.'

The teacher simply accepts the comments without attempting to analyse them at this stage. When the children no longer offer any comment spontaneously the teacher asks them to change over. Again, stressing the need for care, the teacher asks them to walk around the room. After a few moments he or she asks them to stop again and examine what they are doing.

This time, comments are sure to come that,

'You have to trust each other.'
'You feel responsible for each other.'
'You are dependent on each other.'
'It's a two-way relationship.'

This sort of perceptive comment is not unusual even among 11- to 12-year-old children. Although I should not be, I am constantly amazed at the shrewdness of children who can see keenly in a very short time exactly what they are doing.

A point to remember in trust exercises is that we should have established an initial working contract to work together and not to let each other down. The sensitive teacher might elaborate on the theme at this stage by pointing to the language that often comes out of such an exercise: words like,

'You're safe with me; you're in my hands.'
'I won't let you down.'
'You can lean on me.'
'I'm here to lend you a hand.'

It is most rewarding to hear the children quickly matching the metaphorical meaning of such phrases with the physical exercise they are going through. They are always delighted when they can see the immediate significance of what they are doing.

Exercise 2

This is a conversational exercise to help strangers to get to know each other quickly and to develop a sympathetic rapport. The teacher has adopted a 'snowball' technique. The children are in pairs, and as part of the agenda are asked to find out basic information about each other. They need to know names, brothers and sisters, pets, likes and dislikes, and any other minimal information. The teacher pairs up the pairs into groups of four. Now he or she sets the empathy exercise into motion.

The teacher says to Pair 1:

'Now, Edith and Janice, I want you to tell Patrick and George about yourselves. Before you start, I would say that it would be easy for Edith to say, "This is Janice. She has three brothers, a sister, a dog and a cat", and so on. What will make it a little more interesting is if Edith says, "My name is Janice. I have three brothers, a sister, a dog and a cat." If she puts herself in Janice's shoes for a few minutes. Then George can become Patrick and Patrick can become George and tell the girls about themselves. Ready? Go.'

This is a very easy exercise to put into practice, and it can be very rewarding in the amount of personal feedback it supplies, and the degree of warmth generated. It can build a mutual rapport rapidly, and give a firm foundation for the coming session.

Empathy exercises are many. They are exercises which are all designed to enhance the quality of understanding among the children. Any time invested in such exercises will reap rich rewards of understanding, co-operation and trust. The participants will not only benefit from the relationships formed here and now, but they will already be developing the capacity for feeling these emotions in the future.

Personal enquiry

The very best book available on this subject is Leslie Button's *Developmental Group Work with Adolescents* (1974).

Below I return to the basic idea that personal and social education is all about self in relation to others. The whole process of personal and social education is self-centred in the truest sense of the word. That self is seen as the pivot, yet not at the expense of others in society. Personal and social education is not about self-indulgence. It is about living with others, in that symbiotic relationship that results in people happy with themselves and happy with others.

I like the analogy that developed in conversation with a group of colleagues on an in-service course. We were talking about the whole spectrum of personal and social education, and the hierarchical nature of people and organisations concerned with the political aspects of education, as follows:

My colleagues were involved in Action Research and saw the model not as a linear progression but as a global action, with the child at the centre of a circle of pressures and constraints.

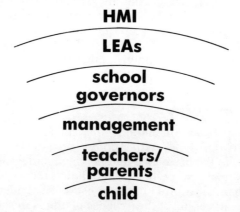

A wit among the group commented: 'It's rather like a gramophone record. We all revolve around the child in the middle.' Then he added as an afterthought; 'Let's hope we keep everything in perspective and make sure he doesn't slip down the hole in the middle.'

PART 3

Logistics

A

Logistics

This section looks at the different conditions and possible constraints that must be taken into consideration when deciding on a scheme of personal and social education. Each school must decide for itself how best to organise and implement its own scheme of personal and social education, taking its own domestic situation as a starting point.

One word of advice remains constant throughout: if one aspect is not working, it should be changed. No staff should ever feel that, once they have embarked on a course of action, they are committed to follow through that action to its bitter end, no matter what the consequences. If something is unsatisfactory, it should go in favour of something else.

Timetable

The first step in planning is to decide on 'the way in' (see section 1B). Is personal and social education to be the responsibility of a particular academic department? Is there to be a social education department specially created, with responsibility for mapping a pastoral curriculum on to the academic? Or is it to have responsibility only for pastoral aspects? Is the school to have a policy of integrated studies, and within that integration are academic and pastoral considerations to have equal status? Is the school aiming for an all-embracing ethos of pastoral care, and is personal and social education an organisational component in realising that aim, or is it an educational framework?

Perhaps the school has rationalised its views on pastoral care and personal and social education, but still suffers from practical constraints. For example, perhaps not all teachers want to be tutors. Has the school a policy concerning this? Is the view that tutorship is compulsory or optional? In our interviews of new staff do we make tutorship a condition of appointment? Have we the resources to provide guidance as effectively as we would want? Have we the support of the governors? What about parental expectations?

These and many more constraints become obvious as the planning proceeds. A solid piece of practical advice would be to look at long-term aims in terms of realising them through short-term means (see section 1A). Even if, for example, we wish to aim for a coherent pastoral curriculum, which incorporates personal and social education across the whole curriculum, we would still have to start somewhere, by putting personal and social education on as a 'lesson' with a legitimate timetabled slot during the school day. In their planning, schools should decide on their long-term aims, certainly, but also identify the practical short-term means by which they can realise those aims. That is the first step.

Having decided on our long-term aims we need to identify how best to introduce personal and social education as an observable part of the curriculum.

The main considerations here are:

1 Which pupils?
2 Which teachers?
3 Which lesson?

1 Which pupils?

Will all classes in the school have a personal and social education lesson or just a few? Selected years, or selected groups within those years? All social and ability ranges or the obviously socially inadequate or poor ability learners?

The choice of which pupils will depend on other constraints of staffing, resources, accommodation, and so on. For example, say the school is just starting off with only a limited number of tutors; clearly the tutors will not be able to cover all the school – although some schools take the decision that this will be the case. All tutors who are prepared to undertake tutorial work and/or personal and social education are given the responsibility for that area throughout the school. This seems a less satisfactory arrangement than if we decide to cut our cloth accordingly and assign those teachers to only a limited section of the school. It depends, of course, on the school's view of how important personal and social education is across the school, whether they are prepared to overload a small contingent for an overall implementation.

The following suggestions might help. Remember that they are suggestions, and not orders, since each school has to take all sorts of variables into account.

a) A whole year group or selected classes in that year: or a whole house group or selected classes in that house?

If at all possible we should aim for a whole year group and not leave anyone out. This will act as a basis for teacher consultation, it will engender team spirit and enhanced morale, and there will probably develop a common core of content. The children will feel involved and identify with each other, particularly if year gatherings are organised, such as assemblies, discos, residential experiences, and so on. Projects may be undertaken by the year or by groups of classes within the year. The year base will provide the framework for the academic and pastoral curriculum. It may also avoid feelings of exclusion from pupils and parents.

Which year or years to select is again at the school's discretion according to its identified needs. Ideally, a school should start with year 1 and take that whole generation through its five or six years; perhaps as more staff join a personal and social education scheme because of new appointments, the following year could start. If staffing is limited it is suggested that earlier years rather than later be selected, and those classes continue throughout the school.

However, there is no reason at all why a school should not start in year 3, 4 or 5. Although it is ideal to aim for a continuum throughout the children's career, there are common elements in personal and social education which may be picked up at any time, and there are also inputs specific to individual year groups. Personal and social education can be successful at any time and with any year group, and, when all is said and done, as short-term purposes dictate, it does not really matter where we start. The important thing is that we do.

b) Children of particular ability ranges? Children from particular social backgrounds?

Personal and social education cuts right across ability, intelligence and social backgrounds. This is an area which is designed to identify with the children, not expect the children to fit into some pre-determined organisational framework.

It is recognised today that all children benefit from personal and social education; it is as important for bright children to get on well in the world as it is for less able children. It used to be part of the repertoire mainly of social workers. This is because personal and social education received popularity and notice because of the credibility given it by the MSC, further education and youth employment agencies among others; but personal and social education has come of age in the secondary sector. Perhaps we are still lagging in terms of the value we give to this form of education, but the gap is rapidly being bridged, and it is starting to receive the attention that it deserves in secondary schools.

2 Which teachers?

Who will teach personal and social education? Will everyone, or just the 'experts'? This can often cause deep difficulties among staffs and be a real block to the organisation and implementation of personal and social education in a school. Teachers get very touchy if they feel that it is not their job, for whatever reason – whether they do not feel confident because of lack of formal skills-training, or because of lack of conviction about the legitimacy of the area, or they do not see pastoral duties as their responsibility, or a variety of other reasons. The fact remains that personal and social education is a sensitive subject in the staffroom and can make hackles rise as quickly as any other area of intimate concern.

Perhaps the most practical piece of advice I can offer to planners is 'never impose'. If elements of personal and social education are imposed, either in terms of the scheme itself as a curriculum innovation, of children to be taught, or of who should teach it, then the exercise can be really counterproductive and lead to all sorts of tensions and hostilities. Schemes can be set back years because of well-meant but ill-handled management. A lot of remedial work has then to be undertaken to get the atmosphere right for people to start to consider personal and social education once again. Time, effort and resources are well invested in planning and persuading for the dividends of goodwill, enthusiasm and conviction.

What is suggested is that the school adopts a long-term staffing policy in relation to planning for personal and social education. In the case of newly-appointed teachers, headteachers can ensure that the appointees are aware of the need for pastoral responsibilities and that they are prepared to take those responsibilities on as a natural part of their duties. If those new appointees have already had professional training in personal and social education methodologies, all well and good; if not, provision should be made for on-going in-service schemes, either school-based or teachers'-centre-based, staffed either by school personnel or advisory services (see sections 3C and 4B on support services).

In the case of already serving teachers, some will be fired with enthusiasm for personal and social education and some will not. Some will be downright antipathetic, and hope to see such schemes fail. They would take a naïve view of expecting to see massive shifts in behaviour from the pupils 'doing' personal and social education, and when those same pupils still manifested unacceptable behaviours and attitudes, those colleagues would say, 'There, I told you so. Waste of time, the whole thing'. It is a question for the individual school to decide whether to invest time and resources on in-service support in an attempt to change such attitudes. Sometimes it is very worthwhile, and many colleagues are prepared to be won over, provided they are given a reasonable rationale, and personalised support from an appropriate professional tutor. At the end of the day, however, some colleagues will refuse to accept personal and social education, and they must be left to their own devices.

In the case of the vast majority of teachers who are keen on personal and social education and willing to have a go, they must be given every encouragement and support. It is strongly advised that schools designate a professional tutor as co-ordinator of in-service support. This may or may not be the same person who co-ordinates the organisation and practice of the pastoral curriculum, including personal and social education (whether this is seen as pastoral or academic). This person should be readily available for immediate support to colleagues, both inside and outside the classroom. He or she should be trusted, and should be in some position of the school management, either middle or senior (see p. 111 personnel). In-service support should be available either in school or based on the teachers' centre. Staff should be encouraged to take part in courses, and benefit from any school-focused support that is arranged in the form, say, of teacher-advisers.

What is to be avoided at all costs is the development of an elite, a band of experts, to whom the welfare of the children is delegated. This is the worst possible move in terms of staff morale and commitment, and can be a really divisive element in the staffroom. This is a danger inherent in a decision to implement several kinds of personal and social education; for example, if one group decides to follow a commercial package, or another designs its own materials, or an enthusiastic group arranges something special without going through all the consultation procedures. Splinter-groups can have disastrous effects on total staff identity and morale. Policy-makers must decide on as cohesive a staffing policy as practically possible, in order to keep tempers even and spirits high.

3   Which lesson?

The trouble about introducing a new area into the curriculum is that everything else must move up a little, or something must go to make room for the innovation. In curriculum planning it is very difficult to find space on an already over-crowded programme for personal and social education.

Often, when schools are deciding on the timetable placement of a new curriculum area, they will try it out on a limited basis. In this case, perhaps an academic department would lose one of its lessons to make way for the new area. Other schools operate their schemes on a withdrawal basis, rotating personal and social education through a curriculum area.

It depends on whether schools see the correct place for personal and social education as a *bona fide* 'lesson' worthy of time within the academic curriculum, or whether they feel that personal and social education should be part of a tutorial system with a prolonged form time arranged, say, at the end of the day or as an extension of registration: or, as some schools arrange, as a part of the break/leisure time when children disperse to year areas within the school building where they are supervised by year staff. If personal and social education is seen as belonging in a less formally structured aspect of the curriculum, it is easier to staff it and to include more form tutors as teachers. If schools decide on this policy they must beware the wrath of systems-minded colleagues who maintain, 'I am now teaching a nine-period day where before I taught eight' or 'I am expected to be teaching when I am supervising'. The answer to this sort of objection is 'Yes, we are responsible for the children at all times that we are in contact with them. We are paid by the child, not by the hour'.

Some schools like to have a double system in operation, whereby tutorial time is arranged for classes to be with their form tutors, say, through an extended registration, and a specific personal and social education time is arranged within the timetable. Staffing would have to be very good for this sort of organisation.

All these questions need thinking about before we put pen to timetable paper. Wise managements will go through a long consultation process at all levels in the school before deciding on a firm policy; and then, having decided, they will make it clear that the door is always open to changes if that chosen system proves unsuitable.

Social structure of the school

This aspect has been well documented elsewhere (Hamblin, 1981; Marland, 1974) and I refer the reader's attention to those books for a detailed survey. In this section we shall look briefly at the main social aspects of schools which have implications for personal and social education.

Most schools, unless they are very small, have some sort of social grouping within the school. This social grouping does not attempt to parallel the academic groupings which are usually well established. The conventional social groupings in secondary schools, taking the model from the traditional grammar schools, were based on a house system. Children identified with the house in academic matters as well as sport, in-school competitions and social occasions. Teachers were allocated to houses and encouraged a spirit of identification among the pupils.

With the advent of pastoral care as a recognised function of the school, the implication was that the social structure reflected the ethos of the school, rather than being in itself a focal point with which the child could identify.

Social groupings in schools tend to follow one of three systems:
a) vertical groupings,
b) horizontal groupings,
c) a co-ordinated mixture of the two.

a) Vertical grouping
In this system the house is the recognised unit and contains representatives from each year group. The social support is spread throughout the school.

Advocates of such a scheme see it as an ideal organisation of care and focused support to each and every child. Through this system children have a wide support system, trusted adults and peers with whom they will go through school.

One of the disadvantages, however, must be that a certain fragmentation might set in. By dividing the school vertically, yet still trying to encourage peer identification, we might end up with as many 'mini-schools' as there are houses. Total group unity might become hazy, though certainly intra-school unity would be strengthened because of the reduced size of the house and the close relationships that are deliberately fostered within the house.

b) Horizontal grouping

In this organisation the year is the recognised unit and contains representatives from each house. The house grouping tends to be reserved for competitive purposes.

The great strength of this system is that it encourages strong peer identity. Barriers of forms and status are eliminated, and children see themselves as members of a school rather than members of units.

It is easily arranged for teachers to take their individual classes within the year right through the school if they wish. Many schools operate some sort of cycle – either year 1 right through to year 5, or a cycle of years 1 and 2, and a separate cycle of years 3, 4 and 5. This is usually to accommodate teachers who are inclined to teaching a particular age-range, or have a bias to younger or older pupils.

The school has to decide whether to aim for continuity with teachers taking their classes through several years. On the one hand it is useful to have a thorough knowledge of the pupils; on the other hand, a change is as good as a rest. People get tired of each other, or too familiar, and teachers of children with special needs are often glad of a change after a year with the same class.

This sort of horizontal grouping is the most widespread among secondary schools, and most of the current literature is in terms of horizontal groupings. The pros and cons of year or house organisation are, however, evenly balanced. There is strength in a horizontal structure which allows identity between the tutor group and the teaching group, but the danger here is that peer group pressures may be reinforced and thereby reduce the influence of older pupils and adults. There might well be a case for building into any school organisation some opportunity for mixed age-group activities so that younger pupils may learn from the experience and greater maturity of their elders. It could even be argued that the horizontal structure places too much weight on the single factor of chronological age and may obscure the vast range of developmental ages to any one chronological age group! These are all factors for schools to discuss in their planning.

c) Co-ordinated year and house groupings

In this organisation there is a dual pastoral system, where year and house groupings are given equal status. Perhaps both groupings have specific responsibilities: for example, the year group will be seen as the focus for children to identify with each other, and for friendships, whereas vertical grouping might be the focus of school-based activities such as fund-raising exercises.

Although no doubt desirable, this organisation would be extravagant in terms of numbers of teachers involved and would take much planning.

It is imperative to hold regular meetings of pastoral heads and their teams. It is suggested that meetings of heads of year/house take place at least once every half term. Those meetings should have an agenda and be minuted, to give status to the meetings in the eyes of the whole staff, and to provide a record of what has been discussed. The head or deputy should attend also, so that all levels of the school are represented and kept informed. Teaching teams, whether year or house, should aim to meet frequently and more informally, perhaps for half an hour once a week.

Let me describe the pastoral system in my own school, Kingsleigh Secondary School in Bournemouth. The prime mover in its development was the headmaster, Mr Alan Macdonald, and he coined the term 'SPACE' programme, standing for Social, Personal and Careers Education programme. The school operates a year system for pastoral affairs, and the house system is reserved for competitions and team sports. It is under constant review, but at the time of writing the programme operates like this:

	Monday 9.00–9.25	Tuesday 9.00–9.20	Wednesday 9.00–9.35	Thursday 9.00–9.20	Friday 9.00–9.25
SPACE time					
SPACE activities	usually administration	assemblies	specific input of PSE	assemblies	specific input of PSE

There is no other time allocated specifically to personal and social education or tutorial aspects, other than in the academic curriculum.

Monday 9.00–9.25 This time is usually given over to administration/ class business.

Tuesday 9.00–9.20 This is usually a school assembly or year assembly/ assemblies. During this time one or even two year-teams of teachers may withdraw to discuss and plan their personal and social education teaching. For example, if it is a full assembly, years 3 and 5 teachers could withdraw. If it is a lower school assembly of years 1 and 2, then the teaching team of year 2 could withdraw and leave the team year 1 to supervise the assembly. The same would take place on Thursday by mutual arrangement among the year heads, so that then, say, year 1 could withdraw. If not that Thursday, they could come to that arrangement the following Tuesday.

Wednesday 9.00–9.35 This time is sacrosanct. It is regarded as specific input time when tutors are with their own groups. Movement around the school, for example, for delivery or collection of homework, is forbidden. The year-teams might wish to assemble so that an aspect of personal and social education may be conducted on a year base, for example, with a film, visiting speaker, school project, and so on.

Thursday 9.00–9.20 This is similar to Tuesday, with school/year assemblies. If the school assembly was not held on Tuesday, it would be held on Thursday.

Friday 9.00–9.25 This is left open to fill in any aspects that have not been covered in the week: a year assembly if necessary, if one was missed during the week, or an activity involving several classes, or further personal and social education. The activity is decided in consultation by year-teams and heads of year, to make sure that everyone knows what is going on. Any spontaneous re-arrangements may be made during the 15-minute staff meeting at the beginning of every day.

With an arrangement like this, time is made for groups of teachers to meet while other colleagues are supervising. Tuesdays, Thursdays and Fridays are deliberately kept flexible to accommodate smaller and larger meetings, and there is a very strong co-operative spirit among teachers. The time is available for teachers also to meet on a house basis, by arrangement with other colleagues. Regular house meetings are also scheduled, usually on Fridays, at least once every half term.

Of course, this is not the only system available, and the system itself is in revision, but this description of Kingsleigh's realisation of a clear pastoral curriculum is representative of how a school can make provision for what it believes in.

Academic structure

There is a vast body of literature available on academic organisations of schools. I shall concentrate only on one aspect that seems particularly relevant to personal and social education, and that is the question of streaming or mixed ability. I use the term 'mixed ability' not in its strictly accurate organisational sense, but to describe a system that is not streamed or banded.

It is up to the school, as ever, to have decided on the placement of personal and social education in the overall curriculum, whether it is an academic departmental responsibility, or belonging in a pastoral 'department' such as social education.

It would seem sensible, in terms of the nature of personal and social education, to attempt a mixed ability grouping for its teaching. The strength of personal and social education is its relevance to the whole ability and social range, and it would seem sensible to let children mix with each other across the board and have experience of levels of ability other than their own. Having said this, certainly we recognise that schools might want to keep certain groups of children separate from the main body. Groups of children with special needs, for example, might be better working separately for their 'practice' sessions, since they need more individualised attention. Or an 'express' group of very able children might get on better working only with each other. The individual school has to decide.

Many schools compromise with a 'moderate' form of streaming. They often have a form of streaming in setting or broad bands of ability, but for lessons which are not academically biased keep more to mixed ability lines. For example, religious education or sports would be on a mixed ability basis. Any section of the curriculum which focused on pastoral aspects, including personal and social education, would take a mixed ability form. We might end up with mixed ability groupings for pastoral time – registration/form periods and tutorials – mixed ability for some academic/vocational subjects – RE, practical subjects, humanities – with a provision for setting if desired, and some form of streaming/banding for academic examination subjects.

Such organisation must be at the discretion of the individual school, but I would recommend that, if at all possible, some form of mixed ability grouping should be adopted for pastoral aspects, for three reasons:

1 All children should have as wide an experience as possible of all ability ranges, social backgrounds and accompanying attitudes, to broaden their focus and expectations of life.

2 Children of lesser ability are not rejected out of the main stream of the school, but are wholly integrated.

3 Children from disadvantaged backgrounds are not relegated to 'lower' streams. Any social stigma is removed.

By the same token it is a good idea, if possible, to do away with form names that suggest some sort of ability or social categorisation. Common practice is to take the initials of the form tutor, or the initial of a surname; 2LF, 3ER, and so on. This is much less damning to weaker ability classes than 2A, 3B or 4C.

By adopting such integrative schemes, schools may modify the association of social disadvantage with lower ability. So often children of less fortunate backgrounds are put into remedial streams because of poor attitudes and behaviour. At least, if we can aim at a policy of integration of all children, regardless of ability, background or attitudes, all children have an equal chance, and each day is a new beginning.

Personnel

Patterns of pastoral systems vary enormously from school to school, depending on their own needs and situations. Such organisational patterns are very well outlined in Marland, 1974. Here I shall outline some elements that are standard to most patterns.

1 The need for a clear structure of personnel

No matter what pattern is adopted, there should be a clear structure in terms of role responsibility and levels of support.

A typical structure would be:

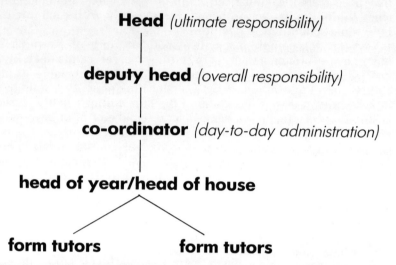

Head *(ultimate responsibility)*

deputy head *(overall responsibility)*

co-ordinator *(day-to-day administration)*

head of year/head of house

form tutors   **form tutors**

This is not the only hierarchy, nor necessarily an ideal, but it is a conventional pattern, showing that the organisational framework specifies levels of responsibility and communication channels.

2 The need for a supportive headteacher

If the headteacher is committed to the notion of personal and social education it makes the planning and implementation of pastoral schemes much easier. If the headteacher is not supportive it is very difficult indeed for teachers to get a scheme off the ground. To make personal and social education operational calls for supportive exchanges at all levels.

It is not recommended that headteachers take on the task of co-ordinating personal and social education within the school, as indeed they would not take on detailed academic aspects. Unless the school were very small, they simply would not have the time. Nor should headteachers be the co-ordinator, because their professional functional roles will be quite different. The role of the headteacher is wide and varied, calling for a broad overview of every aspect of school life in the capacity of administrator/decision-maker, rather than practical implementer. The function of pastoral co-ordinator calls for a much more personalised approach than that conventionally seen as a headteacher's approach; class practice and class support need an intimate, trusting exchange at a personal level, which is not usually the level of dialogue between class teacher and headteacher. Certainly in a smaller school where relationships are very solid and easy such a friendship may be forged, but in most secondary schools such a phenomenon is unusual.

3 The need for a supportive deputy headteacher

Traditionally the deputy is a 'middle' person and has the flexibility to operate at management as well as classroom level. He or she is ideally suited to act as professional tutor/support to curriculum innovations, having the managerial status to oversee their implementation effectively, yet also teacher status to act as a close colleague in class. In terms of a scheme of personal and social education the deputy head would be an ideal co-ordinator, yet may well not have the time to look after the day-to-day administration. He or she may well have to enlist the active support of another senior colleague, say senior master/mistress, or other designated co-ordinator. Certainly the pastoral element in a secondary school ought to be the general responsibility of the deputy but the practical management of personal and social education schemes may well have to be delegated.

4 The need for an able co-ordinator

A profile of a co-ordinator will show someone who:
– has qualities of vigorous, democratic leadership;
– can relate to others easily and show empathy;
– enjoys standing and credibility in the staffroom;
– has sound knowledge of curriculum matters;
– has sensitivity in management to introduce a delicate curriculum area;
– has status of at least head of department;
– has vision, a sense of fun, but is very practical.

5 The need for the right atmosphere

It is possible to meet all the conditions specified so far in terms of personnel, but the most important thing perhaps is the mix. All these people could exist with optimum qualifications to meet all requirements on an individual basis, but if they do not gell as a team, there is no emotional foundation to the exercise. It is rather like a teacher who fulfils all the requirements in this book, yet who has no warmth in the eyes. If the basic warmth is not there, he or she has failed. If the co-operative warmth is not there among the personnel in a school, the system will not realise the planners' aims. Certainly the system will be there, and it will work, but it is the quality of the working that matters, not its operational efficiency.

This quality shines through the life of a school from the top down. It shows in the low number of truancies and suspensions; in the return of children to Speech Day and prize-giving; in the amount of laughter in the classroom. It does not just happen. It is orchestrated by sensitive people who are willing to work together with humour and compassion, who are prepared to put their hearts into what they believe. The mix is all important. If we get that right, the rest will follow naturally.

Size of group and teaching strategies

Personal and social education encourages experiential learning, a personal experience of and commitment to the topic in hand. In order best to effect this type of learning, teaching strategies must rely heavily on personalised approaches that will be immediately relevant and meaningful to the individual and to the whole group. Group work will be a major channel for encouraging this sort of approach with its emphasis on support and encouragement.

For maximum success the teacher–pupil ratio should be about 1:15. The total group should definitely number not more than 20. This is really all a teacher can handle and pay close attention as well. Certainly a teacher can cope with numbers of up to 35 and still get group work going through 'snowballing' techniques and others (see section 2C) but the weight of numbers will cut down on personalised attention, and the teacher's role will be reduced to that of a manager rather than a tutor.

This section deals with the logistics of the teaching situation, and it is recognised that a 1:15 ratio is idealistic and often not practicable for many classroom situations. Often teachers have tutor groups of 30+; and we may well want to adopt this teaching style in our academic lessons, where we may expect as standard a group of 30+. In this case, we have to adopt some sort of strategy of delegation (see section 2C) whereby we appoint a group leader who will substitute for us as teacher.

So from class pattern 1:

where the teacher is managing the total group and able to interact with small groups or individuals within those groups, we arrive at pattern 2:

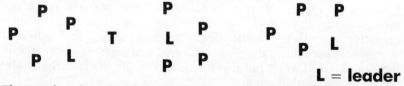

The teacher has divided the larger group into sub-units and has appointed a surrogate leader to each group. That leader is responsible for the management of that group, and the teacher will act as manager of the plenary session.

Clearly the focus changes. In pattern 1, the teacher is closely involved with individuals and may interact personally. In pattern 2, the teacher is distanced from the situation because of numbers involved, and can keep a watching brief. Pattern 1 is very useful for delicate subject matters involving close guidance and help; pattern 2 is adequate for less controversial topics, where the teacher may feed in the basic stimulus and be assured that the pupils may fend for themselves.

If the topic calls for pattern 1, yet we still have to cope with a larger group, then we would have to enlist the help of a colleague and undertake some form of team teaching. This is a case of matching content to teaching style, and it states the need for planning in advance. When teaching teams are planning their schemes of work they will of course make allowances for special inputs which might involve some team teaching and plan accordingly.

There are certain instances when it is imperative to keep the groups as small as possible: groups of children with special needs, or groups of very reluctant learners need personalised attention by their teacher. They would probably find it difficult to accept any sort of delegated responsibility in the early stages, although the fact that they might take on such a responsibility would in itself be seen as an objective. Here again is the notion of the process being at the heart of personal and social education rather than a specific content of information.

The question of size of group has to be resolved within the general framework of school policy regarding staffing, and according to the value that is put on personal and social education.

Resources

We can identify resources in terms of materials and people.
1 In terms of materials and books, the main resources are:
   a) A staff library of relevant material.
   b) Main source books available at least for each head of year/house if money is limited; preferably for each tutor with pastoral responsibility.
   c) Reprographic resources: many commercially available books allow copying of worksheets.

It is always to be recommended that schools develop their own resources. Course books make excellent guidelines and provide ideas and frameworks, but they should never be seen as prime resources. Home-grown resources are relevant and meaningful to the pupils; teachers can tailor their own materials to the needs of the pupils. Having said this, we must always be aware of the need for a high standard of workmanship. Pupils are not motivated by shoddy artwork or printed materials.

Teachers need to be aware of many skills involved in developing effective learning resources, and perhaps one of the implications of this need is for school-based in-service. I would also here make a plea to

LEAs to institute research and development workshops (see section 4B 'Support') which would cater for requests from individual schools to develop ideas and materials conceived by teachers in class. Certainly some teachers' centres already undertake this work to some extent, but it is seldom their specific brief to cater for an area demand for resources or support personnel.

2 In terms of people, the main resources are:

d) Personnel from a research and development centre, such as is to be found at the Resources for Learning Development Unit at Bristol.

e) Teachers' centres as professional centres. These provide the opportunity for open forum, for discourse and professional support.

f) Advisory teachers and schools' advisers. The approach of working at classroom level is to be recommended (see sections 3C and 4B).

g) Time for teachers. Time to think and plan, time for teachers' meetings, time to undertake pastoral duties with the children and their parents or other agencies. Time is sometimes impossible to find; but if a true measure of value is given to personal and social education, then the necessary resources, including time, will be found.

B

Evaluation

A vital part of any innovation is its evaluation. There are a number of evaluation models available in the literature of educational research. Indeed, there are a number of definitions available of the word 'evaluation'. In the whole field of educational research the notion of evaluation is the aspect most under scrutiny, in terms of what it means and how it is done.

This section suggests that we should look carefully at what we are doing in our class practice and be prepared to modify any elements that we regard as unsatisfactory. The process is never seen as that of an expert watching and passing judgement on the rest of us. Evaluation in this book is taken to mean an exercise that the whole school from the headteacher to the pupils may design and take part in, a co-operative effort to monitor the effect that an aspect of the curriculum is having and to bring in any changes that the school feels is necessary. If there is a scheme of personal and social education running as part of the pastoral curriculum, there is a need to see how effective that scheme is in terms of what it set out to do. If we see that it meets its objectives we can look at future progress; if we find out that it is falling short somewhere, then we need to consider how best to improve it.

There can be no doubt of the need to evaluate. It is irresponsible to set a scheme into operation without some sort of feedback. It could be that the scheme is going off at a tangent quite unforeseen by the planners; or that elements are creeping in that ought not to be there; or that people say they are doing things which in fact they are not.

If we accept unreservedly the need to evaluate, we do not accept that there is only one way to do it. Schools are at liberty to try out their own methods, based probably on the information available from educational research. At the moment educational research is in a state of stormy evolution, and evaluation is often found at the eye of the storm. Traditionally, research was seen as a fixed exercise, usually based on the disciplines of the sociology, psychology and philosophy of education. Evaluation was seen in terms of educational objectives: a teacher could suggest what his children would be able to do at the end of a lesson that they could not do before, and if they showed that they could do those things, then the lesson was a success because it had achieved its objectives.

Action Research project

The Action Research movement that is very much in evidence in the 1980s takes the view that research ought to involve both researcher and 'researched' in the exercise. It is unrealistic to do research ON people. It is more true to life to do research WITH people. For an introduction to Action Research the reader is referred to the bibliography on pp. 165, 166.

Not enough research is being done into personal and social education. It is an area heavily value-laden and difficult to evaluate. One of the reasons for the difficulties is that not enough thought has been put into attempting to define personal and social education. We still have not enough real evidence to show how personal development takes place, or what it looks like. These are enormous questions, and their implications are far reaching, not only for schools' schemes of personal and social education, but also for the curriculum itself; for the sooner we can define the criteria that tell us that personal development has taken place, the sooner we shall be able to outline the best strategies to achieve that personal development.

As yet these questions go unanswered. We are hoping, through the work at present undertaken at the University of Bath, to make some progress in providing these answers, and I would gladly enter into correspondence with colleagues who are similarly concerned. It would be sensible here to outline the research project that began in 1981 and continues to date. It is fully documented (McNiff, 1983) and the reader is referred there for a comprehensive but academic treatment of the subject.

I must stress that the following is a brief summary. The research is now in its fourth year, has involved the staffs of several schools, and has a much wider focus than the summary offered here. The model presented is not the only one available, but it was the most appropriate one for our purposes.

I was involved in the development of the Kingsleigh SPACE programme. I was also interested in the work of Dr Leslie Button at the University of Swansea, particularly with reference to his methodologies of personal and social education. I was experimenting with changes in my own class practice for various reasons outlined in a moment, and I was keen to find out about anything that would help me in my practice. Leslie Button's ideas seemed a possible answer.

I put those ideas into practice in my classes, particularly focusing on a group of 14-year-old reluctant learners. As soon as I started doing so I began my evaluation. This exercise was concurrent with the total school SPACE programme, so I was undertaking a gradual process: I wanted first of all to evaluate my own schemes of work and then see how that matched against the practice of the whole school.

I took as my starting-point the fact that some of my educational values were being negated in practice. For example, I wanted the children to be tolerant of each other and sensitive to each other's needs. They were often rude and aggressive. I wanted relationships in class between teachers and children, and between children and children, to be easy and courteous. This was not always the case.

My problem was how I could change things so that my educational values could be realised: so that children would be sensitive and tolerant, relationships in class would be happy and easy, the children would genuinely enjoy coming to school. I focused on my own class as representing this denial of my values. There were 12 children, 14-year-old reluctant learners, girls and boys who were aggressive and rude to each other and to their teachers.

I worked with these children for three hours a week under the general heading of 'English' but in fact our lessons took more the form of focusing on communication exercises and establishment of relationships at first, and later developing into a general studies session when we talked about everything and anything that was important to them.

My evaluation exercise was to find out if I was being successful in my teaching. But what was 'successful'? What criteria could I employ to say whether I was being 'successful' or not? It was not the same as conventional English, with a mark for an essay or a percentage for comprehension. I was evaluating my lessons which dealt in attitudes, emotions, feelings, relationships, values. How could I evaluate those in terms of the psychology, philosophy and sociology of education?

I took as my criteria four starting-points:
1 My personal views of what life in school ought to be like and what I hoped to achieve through my educational practice (my educational values).
2 The stated aims of education by the secretaries of state (see p. 153) HMI:DES, 1981 (national educational values).
3 The stated aims of education by the Education Committee of Dorset LEA, 1981 (county educational values).
4 The stated aims of education by Kingsleigh School, 1981 (school educational values).

They all matched, not surprisingly, in their acceptance of the broad aims of educating for lively, inquiring minds, a compassionate view of one's fellow human beings, and a belief in democracy and freedom of mind.

I had a firm foundation for the *what* of my evaluation. The 'content' of my evaluation was whether, because of my teaching, the children were getting any nearer to a living-through of those values.

It is necessary to digress here for a moment to comment again (see section 1B) on the question of teaching values. One of the hesitancies among teachers is the question of imposition of values. Whenever groups of colleagues speak about the aims of our school practice, they always worry: 'But aren't we teaching values to the children?' My response is Yes, we are, but we are doing more than that in personal and social education. Yes, we are teaching values, the same as we are doing in mathematics, English or car maintenance. We are certainly operating within our own and the school's value system; usually our values match those of the school. We insist, for example, on courteous behaviour, democratic discussion, intelligent involvement, responsible attitudes. We do not believe in aggression, apathy, negative attitudes. We believe in a society founded on care and a school practice grounded in tolerance. We are not ashamed of these values. We stand on our principles and fight to defend them. We are trying, in the whole of our professional lives, to get these values across to the children.

Personal and social education is the classroom practice-ground for an accelerated, intensive exposure to those values. Through the practice of personal and social education we can demonstrate those values to the children, and we can let them see the outcomes, usually in terms of an enhanced quality of life.

Through personal and social education we can help the children go through the decision-making process and to choose appropriately and, if possible, without detriment to others.

So it is a two-step process:

1 We demonstrate a value system to the children and invite them to try it out. There is no compulsion on them to accept those values, although naturally we could point out that there will probably be an enhancement to their own lives; for example,

– if you adopt a polite attitude at a job interview you are more likely to get a job than if you are rude;

– If you are a careful road user you will not cause harm to yourself or others.

2 We point out to the children that everyone has to decide for themselves in life, and we help them to learn how to decide; for example,

– given this situation and bearing in mind all the circumstances, what are the likely effects if you take action course A rather than action course B?

Personal and social education does not seek to impose values. Rather, it clarifies situations, and raises to a conscious level aspects of values that perhaps previously had been unclear. Our whole educational system is value-laden; personal and social education is clarification and practice. It is a liberating exercise, rather than an imposition, and we should never back away from such a challenge.

I return to my evaluation. Having developed a reasonable idea of what I was going to evaluate, I had to determine how I was going to do it. By this time I had joined the University of Bath as a part-time research student and came into touch with Jack Whitehead. Together with Stephen Kemmis he is at the spearhead of Action Research, nationally and world-wide. He has developed a model which is ideal for problems of practical class issues, and I gladly used it at his suggestion.

Model for dealing with issues of class practice

1 I experience a problem when some of my educational values are denied in practice.
2 I imagine a solution.
3 I implement the solution.
4 I evaluate the solution.
5 I modify my practice in the light of that evaluation.

I applied this model to my own practice: (Whitehead, 1983)
1 My problem was that the children were behaving in a way that was unacceptable to me. They were rude to each other and to me. I could not teach; they actively prevented me from teaching.
2 I imagined a solution. I learned about personal and social education and its accompanying methodologies. For example, I felt the work of Leslie Button was particularly relevant and useful.
3 I implemented the solution. I started off a scheme of personal and social education with my fourth years and adopted appropriate methodologies, including a collaborative relationship.
4 I evaluated the solution. It seemed to be working in general, as verified in my validation procedures, in terms of different attitudes and behaviour.
5 I modified practice continually to get the best atmosphere and behaviour from the children. If one aspect of my practice did not seem to be so effective, I changed it and tried something else, continually following the problem-solving strategy.

I recorded the attitudes and behaviour of my children at intervals. I captured them in action on audio and videotape, and kept a careful record over a period of nine months. This record shows a maturing of the children and a growth in sensitivity and an awareness of the needs of other people. From antisocial, hostile children, as shown in a video film of the group three weeks after we began our work together, in six months they were seen to grow into considerate, caring young people. The films make part of the research project, and I keep them as evidence I have gathered in support of the claim that through my class practice I have enhanced the quality of life for the children in my care.

Because of my developing interest and involvement in the field, I was seconded to the local teachers' centre in Bournemouth to help local schools in setting up their schemes of personal and social education. One of the teachers at Oakmead School for Boys, Phil Corbin, was very keen to evaluate his work, and we worked together with his group. They were a first-year group of 11-year-old boys of lower ability. We worked together over a period of nine months. Phil took as a starting point the fact that his educational values were being denied in practice, in that the children were very intolerant of each other. He wanted his children to develop the qualities of compassion and understanding that would lead to an overall atmosphere of tolerance. He saw my involvement with the school as an opportunity for him to try out methodologies which seemed to him a potential towards realising those qualities.

Again we recorded the action of the class. We made films of varying lengths at intervals over the nine months. Slowly we built up profiles of the children individually and collectively, so that we could point to movement that was taking place. We attempted now to define the criteria in action of what we saw as personal development. For example, Peter was a severe stutterer. As time went on he stuttered less when he was with the class. This improvement in his speech could, of course, be attributed to any number of factors. We have it on videotape, however, that Peter talks to Phil about his speech difficulties, and says, 'It's because the other boys help me that I don't stutter in tutorials.'

Equally significant was the increasing confidence of John who, in the early days, was always shouted down and ridiculed because of his deprived background. John was a willing victim, expecting and accepting that this was his lot in life. Phil identified this as a definite barrier in John's realisation of his full potential. He worked with John to increase John's self-esteem and focused in class on aspects of group support. Over the months our records show John's development of confidence, his taking an authoritative place in the whole group. On videotape we have the comments of the other children on how John has matured in tutorials.

We were aware of criticisms that could be levelled against our work and that could threaten the integrity of our claims, that we were actively enhancing the quality of life for these children. We were also aware of the need to include colleagues as intimately as possible with what we were doing as an on-going evaluation of our work. We were happy to hold our work and the results open to public scrutiny and debate. The very openness of our evaluation design encouraged the participative approach we had hoped for. We involved teachers, headteachers and advisers, a visiting county officer, parents. We arranged visitors for the children, both to teach the children the skills of coping with stranger adults, and for our visitors to see our work. We also videoed these sessions; the children coped well with their visitors, and they in turn enjoyed the experience of meeting children in an atmosphere of open discussion.

We were very careful with our validation procedures. We arranged validation meetings at intervals to keep interested parties informed of progress and to agree on the results of our work. A typical validation meeting would include a group of three to ten people, who were all connected with or interested in the project. We showed the results of our work in our films and in the real class behaviour, as well as in our audiotape recording and written reports, as evidence to substantiate our claims. For example, we might want to point to a significant development in the tolerance rating of some of our pupils. We would present the evidence – a video film, an audiotape recording and its tapescript – and we would draw the attention of our validation group to those aspects that we thought significant. The groups were perhaps the most critical of any audience that we could have found, so there is a very vigorous control of the results that we claimed.

After nine months we were pleased to say that our children had made significant movement, as they were pleased to tell people, and as our validation groups agreed.

A second element of the research was my function as worker/ researcher in schools. If my first research question focused on the children:

– How can I, as a teacher, enhance the quality of education for the children in my care?

my second question focused on the teachers:

– How can I, as a worker in a school, enhance the quality of educating for the teachers I am working with?

Again through a process of vigorous validation of the evidence I submit in support of my claims, I can say that I lent in-service support to the teachers that really contributed towards an enhancement of their professional lives.

I emphasise that my research continues. I am currently investigating the criteria in action that characterise personal development. One main criterion, I would suggest, is the growth of individual autonomy, and I am hoping to demonstrate in practice what this means.

We continue the in-service support for on-going professional development in the Bournemouth and Poole area in a number of ways. One of them is an Action Research group which is an open forum for colleagues, from every educational sector, who feel that they want to look critically at their own practice, and to lend mutual support.

As I stated before, this is not the only model for evaluation. But this sort of approach seems well suited to questions of practical classroom issues, by an emphasis on making the teacher the researcher. We took the view that none of us was an expert. We followed a simple, common-sense procedure, we asked our own questions which were pertinent to us, and we discovered our own answers.

Another strength of this approach is its encouragement of a collaborative element. In all the schools where I worked, the fact that we were working together on a new project brought us closer together and provided a forum for talk.

Action Research is parallel in its philosophy to that of personal and social education. Both encourage an openness of exchange; a democratic view of people working together, all with valid opinions, rather than the traditional view of unilateral control by an 'expert researcher'. Action Research emphasises the true place of research in the classroom.

We find this project useful in several ways. One is through the enrichment it brings into children's lives through the schools' schemes of personal and social education and the commitment of the staffs to the values inherent in the teaching of personal and social education. Secondly, there is the tremendous amount of staff development that takes place when a group of teachers undertake a corporate venture. Thirdly, there are spin-offs into other areas of the curriculum by involvement of teachers not immediately connected with the scheme but brought into the movement of staff involvement; and finally the project has established an atmosphere of educational debate and supportive co-operation.

I would recommend wholeheartedly any strategy in curriculum innovation or evaluation to be of a participative nature. The model I chose was such a one. There are others. For example, the Open University 'Curriculum in Action' evaluation pack adopts the same notions in terms of content and process. In the evaluation of content, the emphasis is on a step-by-step approach, focusing attention on the everyday practicalities of a real class situation. The questions are:

1 What did the children do?
2 What were they learning?
3 How worthwhile was it?

The next set of questions focuses on the process, the *how* of the exercise.

4 What did I, the teacher, do?
5 What did I learn?
6 What do I intend to do now?

One of the schools where I worked decided to explore this avenue, and we held a school-based course to look at our own educational practices. The course was intended as part of a 'foundation year' in preparation for a formal scheme of personal and social education the following year. Such was the interest engendered that other colleagues joined in later with other courses. The scheme of personal and social education, when it was introduced, had a firm foundation in terms of staff preparation; the atmosphere was right, but that had taken a great deal of preparation and planning.

Evaluation can be stimulating for teachers if it is approached in an appropriate way. I firmly believe that any school-based exercise, including evaluation, ought to be conducted in a collaborative manner. If teachers can be included it will let them appreciate that theirs is a vital role. Feelings of tension will be eliminated. No one person on the staff should be seen as 'the expert'. Certainly one person, or a small team, may be seen as the guiding lights, but their guidance should aim to include as many colleagues as possible.

There is also a very strong argument for inviting a stranger into school in the capacity of organiser, but, again, not as an 'expert'. Any person who has gained such a position will be aware of the need for strategies that encourage collaborative relationships. A stranger can hold a privileged position, inviting a close relationship with colleagues and bringing them together, but always with the built-in safety factor that he or she is not a permanent member of staff, and will disappear when the job is done.

There should be more evaluation and research into personal and social education. Galloway (1983), for example, reports on good practice in schools where effective schemes of pastoral care are in operation, and this seems to be one of the factors in a reduction of truancies, suspensions and some delinquent behaviour. It is this sort of inquiry that publicly lends weight to the arguments for pastoral schemes including personal and social education. He comments on 'the assumption that effective pastoral care and effective teaching were interdependent, since each was logically impossible without the other: effective classroom teaching would depend on understanding the needs of individual pupils; conversely, understanding and meeting individual needs would affect classroom practice.' This sort of evaluation exercise, and the very positive aspects that it makes public, is invaluable in the promotion of good practice, and there should be more of it.

C

Involving the whole school and all relevant agencies

The implementation of schemes of personal and social education in secondary schools involves three factors: organisation, attitudes and content. They are inextricably intertwined, yet for certain exercises we may focus on one discrete aspect.

In this section we focus on strategies of involvement for all personnel. Which personnel are involved will depend, of course, on how the school sees its own needs. For example, some schools might want to inform parents only briefly of what is going on; others may see parental involvement as an integral part of their schemes.

The following suggestions, then, are offered as guidelines for people involvement. The elements of this involvement can be broken down into four categories: school personnel, parents, educational support services, social support services.

The school personnel

Setting a scheme of personal and social education into operation is bound to affect the whole school to a greater or lesser degree. It might involve everyone, if personal and social education is seen as a curricular framework, or it might involve only a small proportion if the scheme is kept fairly isolated. It will affect the children who are being taught through the scheme, and the teachers involved. At the simplest level, lines of communication must be effective, to let colleagues know what is going on.

I have already pointed to several factors regarding staff involvement which will significantly affect the overall success of a scheme. The atmosphere must be right, and this readiness is brought about by careful planning and considerate handling of professional aspects – staffing, delegation of responsibility, in-service support, and so on. There should be a clear policy statement about pastoral as well as curricular aspects. There should be a great deal of consultation in the form of informal talks at staffroom level as well as scheduled meetings which are minuted and the records made public. An atmosphere of intelligent debate should obtain. All these atmospheric conditions are brought about by skilled managers, and to the managers themselves these skills do not always come naturally. They too must learn their art, and appropriate in-service and support agencies should be available for them as much as for class teachers.

Schools where I have worked have often found it helpful to let others know what they are doing by carrying out a plan of inviting representatives from all departments to visit the groups of children. This achieves two goals; it involves a great many staff from all school areas, lets them see the sort of work undertaken in personal and social education, and gives them a starting point for discussion. The second reason for doing this is that the children learn to cope with adults from all walks of life and get to know people right through the school – the dinner ladies, secretaries, technicians, as well as teaching staff.

Another very useful way of keeping people informed and involved is to arrange departmental presentations. This was a popular strategy of one large secondary comprehensive where I worked. We set aside Monday from 3.45 to 5.30, for workshops, and attendance was entirely optional. Ancillary as well as teaching staff were invited. It was arranged that a special area would receive attention each week, either a special content area, or a progress report, or an area of special concern such as high absenteeism or poor public examination results.

Whichever method is evolved, the main focus stays the same: it is imperative to let people know what is happening and try to include them actively. People who have a personal stake in things will hope to see them succeed, and will work towards that success.

Parents

Schools often find it an invaluable asset to gain the support of parents, particularly in the field of curriculum innovation. In personal and social education it is priceless. Besides the aspect of parental support it is imperative to inform parents about any scheme of personal and social education, simply because they might hear about it from other sources and misunderstand school practice or, worse still, school motives. For example, it is common practice for schools to send home an explanatory note to parents about courses planned on sex education, drugs or alcohol information. This note informs parents briefly about what is intended in those lessons, and invites parents to contact the school for further information. A worried mother of a second-year girl came to see me since her daughter was going 'to receive sex education in her coming third year, and what did that involve?' I was able to go through our whole personal and social education programme with her, show her exactly what was involved in the sex education component, and point out how that fitted into the whole programme.

To supplement this it is a good idea to arrange special parents' evenings dealing with specific areas of the curriculum. At Kingsleigh School there is a policy of arranging evenings dealing with special issues of a curricular or social nature. We arrange talks on drug and alcohol abuse, how to cope with adolescent children, how to help children with their homework, new maths for parents, computer evenings for parents, reports on field trips and residential experiences, and so on, not forgetting personal and social education. These parents' evenings are conducted in the same participative spirit as personal and social education. For example, we arrange group work among the parents, we let them experience for themselves trust exercises, empathy exercises. We invite teachers to be visitors to small groups of parents. We show video films of the children in class, and we talk about the sorts of behavioural results we would hope to see.

When we first introduced our schemes, we started with first-year children. On the new intake parents' evening we told those parents about our curriculum and made special mention of our personal and social element. We pointed out that one of our teaching objectives was to help pupils develop confidence with adults. To this end we had invited our then first-year pupils to act as guides to groups of prospective new parents. The reaction from the parents was gratifying, and they emphasised their wish for their own children to take part when they joined the school.

If parents appreciate what the school is trying to do in creating an atmosphere among the children for the development of personal competence, the chances are significantly increased that parents will work as well from home. In the research project I outlined, we made it a point to inform parents of the classes involved about our hopes and aims. Our purpose in doing this was quite rightly to keep parents informed and involved, but also to arrange for feedback from parents about attitudes and behaviours of the children. A classic comment came back to us in a questionnaire, reading, 'I don't know what the teachers are doing to him, but whatever it is, please keep on'.

Some schools also adopt the policy of inviting parents into the lessons if they feel that it would be useful, but this is not widespread practice because of the possible embarrassment to children and to staff. Certainly it is useful to enlist parents' help in the general pastoral curriculum, as, for instance, as drivers of minibuses on field trips, or as extra supervisors on residential or work experiences. Some schools welcome offers from parents to help with supervision in class, such as extra reading and library services, but these offers of help must be treated diplomatically because of the view of some professional associations.

Whatever the reason for involving parents it is important that we do. They can be a great support, not only in terms of an active encouragement from home in support of what is being undertaken in school, but also in the sense that, if a child knows that parents and teachers are talking together and working together, they are probably taking the whole thing quite seriously. So he or she had better do the same!

Educational support services

It is in the school's interest to take advantage of all the help they can get. It is always a good idea to ask for help, since agencies will not know automatically what the needs are of individual schools. A detailed account of the type of educational support services is given in section 3B, but I shall outline the main ones here.

Advisory service

The advisory service is a powerful ally to schools' development of schemes of personal and social education. Some LEAs recognise the central place of personal and social education in the curriculum and have acted accordingly, providing resources which are proportionate to the value they attach to this area: for example, Devon LEA's appointment of a field officer. The advisory service takes the form of an overall watching brief specific to a small number of schools. In this second case the agent would probably be a teacher-adviser, and this form of advisory support is much more appropriate, I feel, to the nature of personal and social education in a secondary school than the more diffuse support of a county adviser. The teacher-adviser has the power to take an authoritative role in a school and to lend very close and continual support, actually working with colleagues in class, usually in the role of assistant.

Personal and social education is a curriculum area that is unsettling for teachers; they constantly need reassurance of the value of their own class practice; they need someone to put them in touch with colleagues, someone to call meetings and review progress and provide encouragement; they need an authoritative ally in class who says, 'That lesson was good; let's look at ways in which we can develop that theme, or try that strategy, or help that particular child'. Teacher-advisers, or a new-style peripatetic adviser who can lend focused support to a particular school on an intensive or extensive basis are an invaluable asset.

Educational welfare service

Traditionally educational welfare officers have been seen in the light of a truancy service. More recently their role has widened, happily, to be a link between school and home in pastoral and social matters.

Some schools have a policy of encouraging home visits by school personnel, but there are certain disadvantages to this practice. It is unwise to allow teachers of less than head of year/house status to visit homes for all sorts of reasons. One of the reasons must be time; pastoral heads will probably not have the time, as is true of deputies or senior masters/mistresses, whose authority and refined personal qualities would also allow home visits. The usual pattern of home–school communication is for parents to visit schools, either on a special parents' evening, or by individual appointment.

This is where the Educational Welfare Officer can really help. He or she can act as liaison officer between home and school, and this service is very welcome. It is unfortunate that EWOs are sometimes seen in a negative light by many school managements, who seem determined to keep their view of EWOs as truancy officers. National initiatives emphasise the widening brief of EWOs, and some authorities include the EWO as a permanent member of the ancillary staff in schools. They can serve a very valuable function here, again in a role of 'middle man', in that some children will not see them as part of the teaching staff and might choose to relate well to them. By careful management of such situations in schools, EWOs can actively assist pastoral staff in the integration or rehabilitation of difficult pupils into the main stream of school life. This is a service by EWOs which should be welcomed and used by schools.

It is up to the school to enlist the support of the EWO and arrange his or her inclusion into the life of the school. He or she is unlikely to press services on to a school if he or she feels that such an overture will not be welcomed.

It is encouraging that the educational welfare service gives training in personal and social education philosophy and methodology. EWOs may converse authoritatively with teaching staff and, by invitation, take an active part in curriculum planning. We always invite our EWO to our new parents' evening, to let the parents know that the service exists and how they may benefit. We also invite our EWO to our school in-service workshops so that we may benefit from his expertise. He is a great source of information, not only about what other schools are doing, how they are doing it, and how we can become personally involved in other schools' schemes, but also in terms of putting us in touch with other agencies. He keeps us informed of social agencies and the services they offer, and will act as liaison officer with them at our request.

National trends are highlighting the more comprehensive brief and training that the officers are expected to undertake, and encouraging schools to capitalise on the service.

Continuing education facilities

There is an increasing national emphasis on the need for a coherent view of an educational system that covers the whole age-range of adolescence, rather than adhering to artificial breaks which interrupt the continual flow of education. Thus we see the introduction of schemes covering the 14–19 range, bridging the gap between secondary schooling and further education.

National initiatives from the MSC are providing vocational courses which are seen as parallel with or incorporated into the present secondary system. The nature of further education seems to be changing radically because of youth training schemes; and indeed secondary schools are feeling the backwash in the numbers of school-leavers who wish to return for a sixth year.

Adult education is taking an authoritative role in providing further educational facilities for school-leavers, and many schools encourage their senior pupils to take part in adult education courses through a release system. Altogether there is a focus on the need for an integrated educational system across the board and across age-ranges.

Personal and social education is central to this movement. In its other name 'Social and life skills' it has been around for quite a long time. In fact, the ideas of group therapy which stemmed from work conducted with learners with behavioural problems grew into this educational movement. It was centred on the 16+ age-range and is an accepted element of further education and post-16 industrial initiatives. Today's trends in establishing personal and social education in schools highlight the fact that the pre-16 sector is lagging behind in providing this sort of personal and social skills training, and there is much ground to make up. This lack is shown in much of the literature aimed at a 16+ audience. McGuire and Priestley's *Life after school* (1981) is one such publication. Its title suggests that social skills training begins only after the pupils leave school.

There is a need for communication between all educational sectors/ agencies and for common policy regarding personal and social education/social and life skills. Such a communication link has been set up in Dorset under the leadership of Mr Ken Iball, County Adult Education Organiser. A committee draws together representatives from all educational agencies, schools, support services and youth services. This gives people an opportunity to share their information and experience, encouraging them to develop their own good practice.

The committee has also arranged demonstrations of their work through open days, or workshop days, to which they invite representatives from industry and commerce. This invitation is always welcomed by those representatives, and again acts as a source of information to them to help them in their employment of young people and in appreciating what the education services are trying to do. We have built very strong links across all sorts of barriers. We have invited representatives from educational agencies and the world of work into our various schools, and many visits and links are set up among the bodies represented. We have established a strong network and it grows from day to day. Certainly this organisation is not the only one of its kind. Schools which have adopted MSC schemes are similarly involved on an extensive scale. The return benefits promise to be significant.

Health education service

This service is very much in demand from schools across the primary and secondary age-range in terms of resources and personnel. Qualified officers are always ready to assist schools in providing texts, posters, study packages, and so on, and operate a very efficient loan service. Their assistance is particularly relevant to personal and social education, which in a way evolved from health education. Whereas in its initial stages, personal and social education was seen as an aspect of health education in terms of relationships and attitudes, the 1980s view is that health education is seen as the 'health and hygiene' input to personal and social education which now provides an overall framework.

Schools welcome their health education service officers, and may arrange for formal or informal talks with the children on matters of basic health education. The health education service tries to promote positive fitness and health care, individual responsibility and decision-making, all of which are included in personal and social education.

Social support services

These services are described elsewhere in some detail (Marland, 1974), but a brief outline is provided below.

Medical services

This includes the school doctor and nurse care. Regular attendances at schools by health care staff ensure a thorough check-up of all children, a service of immunisation against major diseases, and a support service for any individual case of poor health or neglect.

The school psychological service is another close ally in the case of children who are perhaps emotionally disturbed. The headteacher has a list of potentially disturbed children whom he or she refers to the psychological service. The educational psychologist then carries out extensive interviews with the child, his parents, and any other concerned parties, and, if the case merits such action, will then refer the child on to whatever educational support service is next in the chain – child guidance, special education, and so on.

The educational psychologist is generally recognised as a friend of the school and would certainly be someone acting as a link to the pastoral organisation. If there is time, form tutors or year heads may consult with educational psychologists about the individual children in their care.

Social workers

Social workers in an assigned area may well build up close links with schools, in that they handle a number of cases from roughly the same geographical area. They are generally very willing to co-operate and actively seek the school's support in the cases they handle. For example, a representative from the school may well be called in, say, on the case conference of a child who has been a victim of parental violence and who has now been removed to a place of safety. The school's view of the background of the child, his academic and social potentials, his possible future achievements, may well act as a powerful voice in the child's placement.

A number of teachers, sadly, feel antipathetic towards social workers, seeing them as concerned with children's civil rights and not enough with a framework of discipline. It is a shame that not enough provision is made for teachers and social workers to meet and discuss their common problems and hopes.

Social workers in general do an excellent job under sometimes very difficult conditions. It would be to everyone's advantage, particularly the children's, if more provision were made to encourage a greater spirit of partnership.

Careers service

This will be seen as an essential support service to schools' pastoral curricula, and may well provide the input to the personal and social education component. Many schools operate a system within their personal and social education organisation where careers is seen as a splinter element of the scheme; or sometimes it stands as an autonomous department, independent of personal and social education. Most secondary schools, however, tend towards an incorporation of careers into the whole personal and social education scheme, and usually much inter-departmental work is undertaken to promote an awareness of readiness for choice, decision-making, promoting the attitudes appropriate for work, preparation for work experience, and so on. Attention will be paid to presentation of self, self-image and awareness, attitudes to others, interview techniques and conversation skills, and so on.

In some instances the careers service may well undertake the teaching of these aspects within the school timetable to a given group of pupils, say a fourth- or fifth-year group, for a short term. The involvement of the careers service will depend on how they see their task and responsibilities to schools, the expertise of the staff available, and other resources of time and money. If they cannot undertake a specific teaching commitment they will be glad to act in an advisory capacity and will offer help.

The careers service is an invaluable asset. As time goes on and personal and social education is seen as growing in importance through the whole curriculum, perhaps the careers service will find itself involved in lower age-ranges in the school.

Youth service

Youth workers can often have more influence on certain sectors of the children in school than their teachers. Teachers are often seen as first and foremost disciplinarians, whereas youth workers are seen in more relaxed, liberal terms, as people who are immediately 'on the child's side' without any overtones of authority.

Because of the unstructured nature of the youth worker's role, many secondary schools are reluctant to invite them into school and to encourage an active partnership between teachers and youth workers. This is a sad reflection of a breakdown of a potentially useful liaison because of lack of communication. The partnerships developed between schools and the youth service could be very valuable in bridging gaps that exist between the child's life inside school and outside. Bonds of trust could be forged across the cultures of school and local environment to enable children to come to terms with a bewildering world; the cultural gaps as manifested perhaps in teachers' talk and environment talk could be bridged, particularly if the teachers themselves were prepared to go to the youth clubs as visitors and assistants, not in a judgemental capacity, but with a genuine desire to help and enjoy themselves.

Many schools do work hard to encourage links between school and the community, and the youth service can be an invaluable mediating service. Again there is an overwhelming need for talk, through liaison committee meetings, personal encounters, an exchange of personnel and ideas. That means hard work for a long time, but it is well worth the dividend for the children.

D

Assessment

The effects upon our schools of adopting profiling

There is a tremendous need today for wider patterns of accreditation. Current trends highlight the need for strategies other than formal examinations to give a true picture of a pupil's abilities and interests; yet it is sadly true to say that schools still rely heavily on examinations as the main criterion of success for the pupils, as do employers and parents. There is still the conventional emphasis on academic success as being the qualification even for non-academic work, and our employment criteria often seem to be out of touch with reality. In a time now when schools are seriously considering their function and the nature of the education they offer to meet the needs of their children, much thought and energy is being devoted to strategies to assess and report on the total life of the child in and out of school.

The emphasis on academic achievement is tough luck on low achievers, slow learners and individuals of a practical bent or who tend towards an affective style of learning. Their strengths do not always shine in academic-style tests. A system of profiling, keeping personal records on an on-going basis, allows all achievements to be recorded. Students who are gifted socially, emotionally and personally, though not necessarily academically, have their talents recognised. The pupil whose main talent is caring will be judged as proficient in life terms as the pupil who gets six O-levels. Profiling is democratic and fair, taking due note of all aspects of individuals and allowing for individual differences in the assessment process. It is fair also for academically able students, who have not only their intellectual talents recognised, but also have the opportunity to show off their social and personal skills.

The literature on profiling is growing. In particular, I feel, the work of David Garforth has brought to public attention many of the issues involved, and he has developed a practical teacher's manual on *Profile assessment: recording student progress* (1983). He points to some of the reasons for wider patterns of accreditation. Among the list he notes:

The pattern of assessment and accreditation should:	The present external examinations dominated practice tends to:
– provide the student with a full picture of achievements, skills and experiences gained during the period of compulsory education.	– provide the student with a result which reflects the response to a limited area of the cognitive domain at a particular point in time.
– inform the student of areas of strengths and areas of weakness where future education may provide remedial help.	– reflect in a global grade, the particular response. It generally provides no specific information to the student concerning particular weakness or strength.
– provide information for the teacher so that the teaching programme can be evaluated and that individual student needs can be satisfied.	– provide little help for teachers in highlighting areas of the course which have not been taught successfully. The demands of the syllabus make it impossible to diagnose individual student needs and even more impossible to provide remedial attention to satisfy those needs.
– encourage styles of teaching to promote individual growth and the development of a broad spectrum of skills.	– stress factual recall which leads to a style of teaching which does little to encourage objectives of participation, or the development of important skills such as reasoning, discussion, analysis and evaluation.

This is a selection of the points made. The notion of a pupil-centred system of education is reflected in these points. We are led to ask ourselves the questions: 'Who are examinations for? What purpose do they serve? What are they supposed to be examining?'

The new movement of pupil profiling offers an answer to schools who are concerned that the curriculum is relevant and meaningful to the pupils in the school, and that an assessment of their final years will reflect the total pattern of the success of their school life. Pupil profiling offers a shift in focus of an examination system – not only recording the pupil's public examination performance, but also in offering a comprehensive report on personal development, interests, aptitudes, experiences in school and at home, and so on. The profiling movement does not suggest doing away with the present examination system nor an examination focus to academic subjects. It does require us to think in wider terms about the success of the pupil's life in general terms, and how we, as tutors and supervisors, may best contribute to that success.

This brings into focus the point that traditional examinations measure not only how well the pupil has learnt the subject matter but also how well we have taught it. If our pupils' public examination performance is not as favourable as we had hoped, we should look closely at what caused the result, including our own school practice. In the same way, by adopting a continuous assessment strategy we would continually be looking at our own teaching, its content and its presentation, through the necessity of making it meaningful and relevant to the pupils.

Garforth outlines the effects upon our schools of adopting profiling. He comments on the increase in pupil motivation, improved relationships, feedback on teaching, implications for academic curricula and pastoral systems, the implications for society, and so on. His comprehensive treatment of the subject is well worth reading.

The implications of profiling are enormous, particularly in educational and political terms. Profiles may often be used as diagnostic instruments, and, as such, will have an effect on what is being taught in class. The notion of profiling rests on negotiation; if the pupil is to have a say in what he is learning, and how, then teachers need to be acutely aware of what they are doing in their class practice, and why.

Throughout this book I have stressed the need for schools to make their own decisions. I have presented frameworks and pointed out the options, but in the final analysis the school must decide for itself which system to adopt, for only the school knows its best reasons.

The same principle applies with profiling. Having viewed all the evidence and weighed up all the advantages and disadvantages, the school must then make its own decisions whether to adopt a system of profiling in the first place, which system to adopt, whether it will replace or supplement the already established assessment system, and how they are going to conduct the whole exercise.

The school has to decide on:

1 criteria for a profile,
  – what is to be assessed?
  – how?
  – for what purpose?
  – and so on.
2 the design of the profile.
3 the use of the profile.

The school has to accept that a profiling system is going to affect the curriculum and the lives of teachers and pupils. In personal and social education the implications can be quite profound, particularly if the school intends to adopt a 'formative' profiling system, which is a

135

system that records the development of pupils as they go through school. This will bring the role of the tutor into much sharper focus, and, if tutors are to follow each and every child's progress through the school, they must be given sufficient time to do so. Such a system will require much closer links with the child than tutors have time for at present.

An organisational implication is that schools may well see the emphasis for a profiling movement within the framework of personal and social education. A two-way relationship is bound to develop between curricular aspects and pastoral aspects, each influencing the other. The curriculum becomes meaningful to the child because it is a reflection of the skills and aptitudes that he wants to develop, and the pastoral curriculum is the location of that development. It becomes an action–reaction cycle, with the child's well-being and development at the centre, and all resources working towards an enhancement of the quality of his life.

The reader is referred to the bibliography (p. 164) for more detailed work, but I must emphasise these two points:

1 Whether to adopt a profiling system, and which types to adopt, must rest with the individual school.
2 All decisions must be agreed by the whole school. It is imperative, as it is in adopting systems of personal and social education, to involve as many people as possible in the discussion process, and later in the organisation and working of the system. As I have already pointed out, systems which are imposed are likely to fail, for all sorts of reasons, particularly in emotive areas like profiling and personal and social education. We are dealing with the very lives of the teachers, their expectations, their values. It is a fragile process and must be handled with care.

Profiling is a massive subject area. A growing body of literature is available, and in this section we have only skimmed the surface. The ideas and values inherent in profiling are in total sympathy with personal and social education, and if schools are thinking about coherent pastoral curricula, they must take profiling into account.

PART 4

Implications

A

Changing roles

Any new educational wave is bound to have repercussions for all the people involved, not only the children but also the teachers and the schools they work in. This book has looked at methodologies based on a philosophy of education which is perhaps not yet general currency in secondary schools. In adopting this philosophy, teachers are going to find a significant change in their own lives, and in the nature of the schools in which they work. This part looks at those two aspects: the changing role of the teacher, and the changing role of the school.

The changing role of the teacher

So far this book has presented signposts along the way: the ideas of an appropriate teaching style, an arrangement of the conditions of learning to achieve basic teaching principles, teaching techniques and skills conducive to experiential learning, assessment procedures – these are the mechanics of the exercise of leading to the child's personal development.

What of the agent? He or she is the person who is going to put the mechanics into operation, and the task of developing courses in personal and social education is bound to affect his or her role. This must be one of the reasons why teachers are sometimes cautious about personal and social education, for they recognise intuitively that it has major implications for their own role and practice. For example, one of the fundamentals of personal and social education is that of a collaborative relationship, a negotiated class practice. Children are entitled to their say in the organisation and content of the lesson. Where is the authority and discipline of the teacher? Are they not hopelessly undermined?

No, they are not. If anything, they are strengthened. The philosophy of personal and social education would maintain that the authority of the teacher is enhanced through his very management of the learning situation, where he can arrange for a range of experiences for the children and guide them along; the teacher's discipline is enhanced in that strengthened relationships will lead to a strengthened discipline. It will not only be an imposed discipline, it will also be the self-discipline of the children that he or she has shown them that they possess.

There is here a very significant change in the way that teachers see themselves. It is a development, an opening out, an extension of self. From a constrained approach of unilateral controller they become democratic leaders; from dictators they grow into providers. The class-room is not a pre-determined ground of teacher expectations; it is a practice ground for pupils' development.

Teachers are now not only charged with imparting the knowledge and skills relevant to our rapidly changing world, but also have to develop the appropriate organisational skills for establishing the correct atmosphere for the acceptance of those knowledges and skills. They are not only teachers in the traditional sense of passing on concrete information or skills; this role is now widened to a pastoral role which arranges an appropriate social environment as well.

This shift in direction can present a dilemma to teachers who find themselves engaged in schemes of personal and social education. This is an area that calls for personalised support of pupils by the teacher. The activities and exercises that go into personal and social education, the whole direction of personal and social education, calls for us to enter into an energetic, personal relationship with our pupils. For those teachers who are used to a distanced approach to their pupils, this can surely be a traumatic experience. Traditional relationships in the classroom have been those of the teacher telling the children what to do. Most secondary schools' curricula reinforce this notion, with the emphasis squarely on subject specialisation. In fact, in any debate about whether secondary curricula should be pupil-centred rather than subject-orientated, opinions would probably hold that schools ought to move towards a pupil-centred curriculum. Yet the reverse is true of the everyday life of schools; the emphasis is continually on subject special-isation. So often, schools' curricula deny in practice the very educational aims which are their frameworks.

There seems to be a restiveness in the teaching profession about the question of role. Many teachers at grass-roots level seem to want to break free of the role of instructor. There is general acceptance, no doubt brought about by many of the issues already mentioned in this book, that schools must take on the full responsibility for young people's total education, and teachers accept the implication of a much wider brief than has so far been the case. Yet many teachers feel that they do not have the necessary skills nor training, at least not at a cognitive level. They perhaps feel intuitively that they would like to break with the traditional concept of a teacher, to alter their image, but they are hesitant to do so, possibly because there is as yet no accepted alternative model available. There is no positive guidance given in what to do and how to do it.

It is not suggested here that teachers' abilities to impart the skills or knowledge of their subject areas should be any less; it is a real request that their pastoral skills should be more. The responsibility lies on teacher education, either initial preparation or on-going professional development. Departments of education in turn have to accept the responsibility of preparing teachers adequately for the extended role they have to play. Courses must include elements of preparation for school teaching in all its aspects, pastoral as well as knowledge/skills based. It is almost unbelievable that the notion of pastoral care has been articulated and put into practice for years, yet many institutions of initial teacher training are only now slowly putting it as a crucial element into their curricula.

The changing role of the school

If the role of teachers is changing significantly, what of the schools in which they teach? A change also seems to be taking place in the role of the school. Traditionally, teachers have been seen as imparters of specific knowledge and skills, but they are now taking on a wider pastoral role. In the same way, schools still have the job of being centres of instruction, but they have now widened their function to provide a total pastoral environment of love and care.

The underlying ethos of a school can be observed in two ways: through its curriculum and through its physical nature, both a reflection of the school's educational values. The 'content' of education is centred in the curriculum: what is to be taught. The learning environment is seen through the physical geography of the school: the conditions of learning.

The attitudes of the teachers to education will be reflected through the curriculum, provided, of course, that there is a consensus of opinion among the teaching staff. Perhaps there is a strictly academic approach; perhaps a parallel or integrated pastoral approach. Perhaps the academic is juxtaposed on to a pastoral. Whatever may be the case, how the school organises its curriculum will reflect its attitudes and its values.

These attitudes will also be reflected in the physical geography, the environment in which the curriculum takes place; how the school organises its classrooms, where various groups of pupils are located, and how a school arranges for optimum communication between its members. The question of resources immediately springs to mind. It is all very well talking in these fairly idealistic terms, we say, if we are talking about a new, purpose-built school. What about those of us who are struggling along in old-fashioned buildings and split sites? Where does the money come from to help us realise our educational values?

I would suggest two considerations:

1 Schools in even the most archaic buildings can go a long way to realising their educational values, certainly through the curriculum and to some extent through the physical environment. Of course it calls for initiative, resourcefulness and enthusiasm in the face of great odds, but so does teaching.

2 LEAs should accept the responsibility for demonstrating the value of pastoral curricula and their central place to the welfare of the children, and allocate resources appropriate to the realisation of those considerations. This means injecting money into developing present buildings to accommodate activities that are central to pastoral curricula, such as open-plan classrooms and furniture, spaces for year- or house-groups to gather, offices to facilitate communication, and so on.

It would be glib to talk about schools as either academic institutions or pastoral agencies. The good school is both a caring community and an effective teaching organisation aiming at the best possible academic standards. In many schools which have decided on a pastoral policy, there are significant signposts of that policy within their working life and their geography. Some of the signs would include:

Curriculum

- importance of a framework of care and support within which are taught academic subjects and specific personal and social skills.
- integration of subject competence, cross-curricular skills, personal and social skills, achievements and experiences.
- an emphasis on teaching styles that involve the learners and encourage problem-solving strategies.
- assessment through a record of personal achievements (profile) complementary to, or as an alternative to, conventional examination procedures.
- a validation procedure to guide and monitor development and operation of curricular innovation.

Staffing

- clear pastoral structure among tutorial staffs as well as academic staffs.
- lines of discussion involving the school, the LEA, parents and employers.
- on-going professional development in pastoral as well as academic matters.
- regular LEA advisory support, probably in the form of a teacher-adviser and/or professional tutor.

Buildings

- classrooms arranged to encourage open exchanges. Classrooms often grouped in year/house groupings. If classrooms are grouped according

to subject disciplines, e.g. all geography rooms are along one corridor, provision is made for year recreation areas.
– social areas: club rooms, year/house recreation areas, activity areas.
– provision for classrooms to be extended, e.g. with movable dividing screens, to allow for team teaching, larger groups, etc.
– 'humanising' aspects: pictures, plants, etc.
– office space arranged for tutorial/pastoral interviews as well as for administrative purposes.

Most schools find themselves in an evolutionary process when they are taking on the responsibilities of the pastoral care of their pupils, and it takes a long time to make provision for all necessary elements. They still have to retain their function as academic instructional institutions, as well as build an outer framework of pastoral care. A school cannot turn into a socialising agency overnight; it takes time for discussion, planning and implementation of recommendations.

Yet this is the task that secondary schools have to face, to accept that 'the welfare of each child is a major charge on the curriculum'. Schools face slow but sure change, and changes in their very nature. Their function has expanded, as has that of their personnel.

What is lacking is sufficient school-based guidance and support to enable schools to recognise the changes that are inevitable and to help them develop appropriate coping strategies. That support is growing as LEAs recognise the vast implications for the roles of teachers in schools from the increased emphasis on pastoral systems, and I plead for an acceleration of that support.

B

Support

There are two types of teacher education currently available:
– initial teacher education.
– on-going professional development.
and three main types of in-service support:
– LEA support in the form of county or area adviser. It is difficult for an adviser at area or county level to lend focused support to any particular school because he or she has far too many schools and institutions to look after. The pressures and demands are too many, and he or she is forced to take a global view. However, LEA support (see below) in the form of a teacher-adviser is also available.

Advisers will arrange for inter-county/DES regional courses, or in-county courses, arranged usually on a thematic basis. Such courses may be of a short intensive duration, or extensive, on-going over a longer period of time.

– Teachers' centre/professional centre-based. Support through these channels will often be geared to the identified needs of clusters of schools, usually on an area grouping arrangement. Organisers/tutors of such courses may be local teachers with an expressed interest or expertise in a certain curriculum area or teaching/support strategy; the advisory service; support from local universities or institutes of education. Perhaps the teachers' centre will enjoy a brief for lending in-service support to schools on request; perhaps an advisory teacher will be based at the teachers' centre with a brief to assist schools in whatever way they request.

– School-based. This support will be strictly relevant to the school's needs. They will have the opportunity to identify needs as they see them and imagine appropriate solutions. The support agent will be on hand to assist in the implementation of those solutions, and in their evaluation, and in any discussion about modified practices as the evaluation indicates.

The agent responsible could be an LEA area adviser, but his or her time will be limited, simply because there are so many schools to be responsible for. Another agent could be an advisory teacher, or teachers' centre-based agent, who will be able to spend time actually in class in the school and in discussion with teachers, individually as well as collectively.

Alternatively the school might like to appoint its own professional tutor, probably a person from senior management, with a specific responsibility for on-going professional development and pastoral care for teachers.

Pastoral support systems should be available as much for teachers as for pupils. Schools are accepting their responsibility for the welfare of their pupils, and making provision through their curricula for those responsibilities. Pastoral support for teachers is lagging behind. It is often this lack of support that accounts for recalcitrance on the part of schools to adopt schemes of personal and social education because of the difficulties in rationalising such an emotion-based area or because of the lack of clear criteria of guidance. Schemes of personal and social education are further threatened by colleagues who are insufficiently aware of their own capabilities in the first place, or who find the going a little too arduous and drop out. Support must be provided, and on a personalised basis.

I would put forward some recommendations which, in my view, would greatly assist in ensuring pastoral support for teachers in schools and an enhanced quality to their professional lives with, by implication, a more efficient system of personal and social education and an enhancement in the quality of education for the pupils in their care.

To use the problem-solving strategy referred to earlier:
1 identify the problem
2 imagine a solution
3 implement the solution
4 evaluate the solution
5 modify practice in the light of the evaluation

Identify the problem

1 Identify the needs of schools; do they need help in:
– rationalising personal and social education?
– getting the atmosphere right?
– persuading colleagues?
– encouraging discussion?
– and so on.
2 Identify the needs of teachers; do they need help in:
– clarifying their own ideas about personal and social education?
– encouragement to look critically at their own class practice?
– developing their professional expertise?
– identifying the needs of the pupils in their care?
– and so on.

3 Identify the needs of the pupils; do they need help in:
- coming to terms with the expectations of the school?
- coming to terms with the expectations of parents?
- working together with peers, teachers and other people in authority?
- and so on.

Imagine a solution

The process by which teachers imagine a solution to their various identified needs is often best accomplished through discussion with other involved parties. This discussion is essential in pastoral matters, since the exercise of implementing any solutions is bound to involve a number of people. The welfare of children cannot happen in isolation; it is not specific to any one person, place or time. It involves anyone who comes into contact with that child. Policies should be formulated by discussion and agreed solutions.

Consultation at all levels is imperative, and there should be an emphasis on supportive comments, to enhance the self-esteem of everyone involved in the discussions. Consultation of all agencies is desirable, from parents as well as from support and educational agencies. The more actively involving, the more far-flung the communication network, the likelier are the chances of acceptance and efforts to ensure success.

In terms of setting up support programmes for teachers in schools there should be at least three stages:

1 A planning stage, where ideas may be discussed, possible strategies for implementation, and support.
2 An implementation stage, where ideas discussed during the planning may be put into practice.
3 A follow-up stage, not quite into evaluation, but lending every encouragement to the success of the programme. If this follow-up is not provided for, schemes may well fold through lack of conviction, enthusiasm or momentum.

We discovered in our LEA that schools tended to be like aeroplanes in their continuing schemes of personal and social education. If there was intensive initial support, but that support was withdrawn, a school that had already gathered sufficient momentum tended to carry itself along; those who had not, tended to run into difficulties fairly soon and, sadly, some schemes fizzled out. Then there was a need for a quick injection, a blitz programme of remedial support.

The three stages are interdependent, and none should be omitted in the cause of economy of resources or manpower.

Implement the solution

The implementation of a support system for teachers in schools should be as personalised as possible. This is essential for teachers in pastoral areas, including personal and social education, but is also becoming

145

more and more necessary for teachers in academic subjects, since the shift is taking place to ensure that academic subjects are taught against a general pastoral backdrop. I would suggest a hierarchy of support for the dissemination of good practice.

Pattern 1

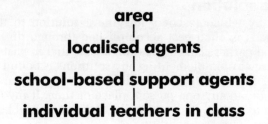

area
|
localised agents
|
school-based support agents
|
individual teachers in class

The need for and function of the first three layers of the support hierarchy are outlined above (pp 138, 139, 140). I have also indicated that, in addition, teachers in class have the greatest need of all for a personalised support by a caring colleague, yet it is this level of professional support that is most absent. New-style advisory teachers are taking on this role, however, actually conducting training sessions in class. For personal and social education it calls for a special type of agent who is well aware of the need to employ problem-solving strategies to enable teachers to discover meanings for themselves. Personal and social education calls for a personal involvement and commitment by practising teachers; and the most efficient way in which they may develop insights into enhancing their own class practice is to engage critically in that practice.

Pattern 2

In pattern 1 the emphasis is still on centralised control of a dissemination programme. It follows the notion that there are 'experts' who are trained, develop the necessary expertise, and are sent into schools or other levels of the professional community. Such agents are responsible to a central authoritative body. A new style of support for professional development would be to involve teachers in their own or in other schools; to promote the idea of the teacher as the expert.

Similar patterns of training could be developed: at area level there would be a central dissemination agency, organised probably by the advisory service. Such a gathering would invite class teachers to attend and go through an experiential training similar to that for children in schools, so that the teachers themselves would develop insights into the practice and philosophy of personal and social education.

The organisation of the dissemination process would then probably be that teachers returned to their own schools with a view to putting into practice with their children what they had learnt, and also to involve and share insights with colleagues.

This is where localised agents are necessary, and school-based support agents; people from the central agency will be welcomed into teachers' centres and into individual schools to work with groups of schools and with groups of teacher trainers.

Also relevant to this discussion is the need for resources and materials which are appropriate to the individual school's needs. At present the most available source of materials are commercially produced training manuals (Button, 1981; Baldwin and Wells, 1981; Thinkwell, 1979). What is needed is provision of specifically designed materials as requested by class teachers in their own schools. I would like to see locally based research and development units with easy interchange between development officers and teachers in class. Officers from such units would be available to go into schools by invitation to talk to teachers and try to meet their requirements in the production of suitable materials. Reciprocal arrangements could be made for teachers to visit or contact the unit with a request for materials. The officers would also be available to evaluate the use of developed materials in schools jointly with the teachers who are using them. This system already operates in some places, for example, the Resources for Learning Development Unit in Bristol, and we can only hope to see more of them.

Evaluate the solution

It has been suggested in this book that probably the most productive form of evaluation of school and class practice is by engaging in a collaborative exercise.

If we are evaluating the support to teachers engaged in pastoral schemes, we have to go through the process of identifying our aims and seeing how far our practice goes towards realising those aims. The aims themselves will be based on an identified need. So we arrive at the scheme:

1 I experience a problem when my educational values are denied in practice.
   - I need to rationalise my ideas on personal and social education. I need advice from someone else.
   - I need help in devising strategies to get co-operation from the children in my groups.
2 I imagine a solution to the problem.
   - I will try to find help – from advisers, our advisory teacher, colleagues.
3 I implement the solution.
   - I ask a colleague or the adviser to come into class with me.
4 I evaluate the solution.
   - How far is the support action assisting me in realising my educational values? Are my ideas any clearer? Am I getting more co-operation from the children?

- Is the quality of education being enhanced for the children because of my involvement?
5 I modify practice in the light of the evaluation.
- I change course or strategies if things are not working. I start again by identifying where things are going wrong, and I take appropriate remedial action.

It has also been suggested throughout that the best and most productive type of support is that of mutual working together in schools. School-based training schemes are best, since they will be immediately relevant and meaningful to the children within those schools. By adopting a school-focused scheme, it is also possible for schools to build in their own criteria for good practice, such as the basic principles mentioned in this book. They can set up workshops and training sessions appropriate to achieving those criteria.

Then, at a further stage, teachers may work together on an evaluative basis, seeing how far their practice matches their aims.

Trends point to an emphasis on school-focused training programmes. Teaching perspectives are widening from instruction to education; and advisory services are moving from a body of experts, who are prepared to inform and direct, to skilled managers, with all the social skills to support and encourage others to develop their own expertise through their own class practice.

Modify practice in the light of the evaluation

If we find that things are not going as they should, then we should change the relevant aspect of the education that we are encouraging. In terms of achieving educational values, we are continually moving towards our ideal that we hope may be realised in practice.

One of the difficulties, as I mentioned right at the beginning, is that at present there are no generally accepted criteria to characterise the nature of personal and social development which we must view as an outcome of our pastoral schemes. There are recommendations from HMIs and LEAs to help us recognise the sort of areas that we are aiming for; that we hope to enable children to develop lively, inquiring minds, to think for themselves, to develop compassion and sensitivity, and so on, as well as specific knowledge and skills areas. What is needed now is intense guidance for teachers into strategies which will enable them to teach for the realisation of those criteria. Further, more research is needed to demonstrate the realisation of those criteria in action.

Advisory support is essential. In a 1980s' view of education it is focused on the self-education of teachers, by providing them with a supportive learning environment within which they may develop on a personal as well as professional level. School is a learning ground as much for teachers as for pupils.

When schools are evolving schemes of personal and social education they may well find that, in the initial phases, there is probably more teachers' education under way than pupils'. In many ways, personal and social education is a practice ground for teachers in allowing their instincts to blossom. It has a foundation in friendship where teachers may work towards their ideals and realise their true calling as educators.

Bibliography

Section 1
The theory of personal and social education

1 General reference books on pastoral care

Best, R.G., Jarvis, C.B., Ribbins, P.M. (eds) (1980)
Perspectives in Pastoral Care Heinemann Educational
A source book of current thinking in the field. The editors
have directed the only pastoral care unit in the country, and
present a professional discussion of theory and practice.

Blackburn, K. (1975)
The Tutor Heinemann Educational
A very useful book which looks at the role of the teacher in
relation to pupils, in groups and individually.

David, K. (1983)
Personal and Social Education in Secondary Schools
Longman for the Schools Council
Part of Programme 3: *Developing the Curriculum for a
Changing World.* The report is from the Schools Council
working party, seeking to identify common aims and methods,
as well as encouraging a more coherent, integrated approach.

Hamblin, D. (1978)
The Teacher and Pastoral Care Basil Blackwell
This book looks at a skills-based system of pastoral care in
school, and gives advice on teaching children how to cope
with school and the transition to the outside world.

Marland, M. (1974)
Pastoral Care Heinemann Educational
A basic source book covering general aspects of pastoral care
in secondary schools. A very useful book, with practical
ideas on setting up a pastoral curriculum.

Williams, T. and Williams, N. (1980)
Personal and Social Development in the School Curriculum
Schools Council
Part of the Schools Council Health Education 13–18 Project:
a very useful report, pointing out the difficulties of integrating
the pastoral curriculum into the academic.

Also:
David, K. and Cowley, J. (eds) (1980)
  Pastoral Care in Schools and Colleges Edward Arnold
Elliott, J.and Pring, R. (eds) (1975)
  Social Education and Social Understanding University of London Press
Kellmer Pringle, J. (1980)
  The Needs of Children Hutchinson

2 Aspects of moral education

McPhail, P., Ungoed-Thomas, J.R., Chapman, H. (1972)
  Moral Education in the Secondary School Longman
  A valuable source book for teachers, resulting from the Schools Council Moral Education Project, *Lifeline*. There is also a class book, *Our School*, looking at the skills of caring. Well worth reading for teachers setting up their own pastoral curriculum.

Peters, R. (1966)
  Ethics and Education Allen and Unwin
  A classic which should be in every staffroom library. It presents a masterful treatment of the function of education as a context of morality.

Raven, J. (1977)
  Education, Values and Society H.K. Lewis
  An excellent book which requires close study but is well worth the effort. It looks at the issues of personal values in education within the context of social expectations.

Williams, N. (1970)
  The Moral Development of Children Macmillan
  A study which is comprehensive in its treatment of the subject.

Wilson, J. (1981)
  Discipline and Moral Education NFER–Nelson
  This book suggests that much current practice in discipline and moral education runs contrary to the opinions and expectations of society.

Wilson, J., Williams, N and Sugarman, B. (1967)
  Introduction to Moral Education Penguin
  The book attempts to answer the three questions: 1 What is moral education? Who can be said to be morally educated? 2 Which findings of psychology and social science are relevant to it? 3 How can children at school be morally educated? The book requires close study, but it is well worth it.

Also:

Bridges, D. (1980)
 Discussion, Democracy and Education NFER–Nelson

Cox, E. (1983)
 Problems and Possibilities for Religious Education Hodder
 and Stoughton

Hersh, R.M., Reimer, J. and Paolitto, D.P. (1979)
 Promoting Moral Growth Longman

Hirst, P. (1974)
 Moral Education in a Secular Society University of London
 Press

Kupperman, J. (1983)
 Foundations of Morality Allen and Unwin

Mischel, R. (ed) (1974)
 Understanding Other Persons Oxford: Blackwell

Nelson, J.L. (1975)
 Introduction to Value Enquiry Rochelle Park, (N.J.), Hayden
 Book Co

Straughan, R. and Wigley, J. (eds) (1980)
 Values and Evaluation in Education Harper and Row

3 Frameworks for personal and social education

Blackham, H.J. (1978)
 Education for Personal Autonomy British Association for
 Counselling/Bedford Square Press
 This is a very useful collection of papers, pointing to the
 central place of pastoral care in helping to foster pupils'
 personal autonomy throughout their school life.

Denys, J. (1980)
 Leadership in Schools Heinemann Educational
 The underlying philosophy of this book is that leadership in
 schools is a shared, democratic experience, and the book
 covers the different concepts of school frameworks which
 contribute to this style of democracy.

Department of Education and Science (1980)
 A View of the Curriculum HMSO
 This brief paper is a useful introduction to:

Department of Education and Science (1979)
 *Aspects of Secondary Education in England: A Survey by
 HM Inspectors of Schools* HMSO

Hamblin, D. (ed) (1980)
Problems and Practice of Pastoral Care Basil Blackwell
A valuable book, looking at the skills involved in pastoral care, as well as discussing specific problems of adolescents.

Poster, C. (1976)
School Decision Making Heinemann Educational
This book looks at frameworks and styles of leadership, and stresses the need for open and effective communication as a basis for successful school management.

Pring, R. (1984)
Personal and Social Education in the Curriculum Hodder and Stoughton

Also:
Department of Education and Science (1977)
Curriculum 11–16 HMSO

Department of Education and Science (1983)
A Framework for the Curriculum HMSO

Department of Education and Science (1981)
The School Curriculum HMSO

Department of Education and Science (1980)
Special Educational Needs (The Warnock Report) HMSO

Jennings, A. (1978)
Management and Headship in the Secondary School Ward Lock

Moore, B.M. (1976)
Guidance in Comprehensive Schools NFER

Schools Council (1981)
The Practical Curriculum (Schools Council Working Paper 70) Methuen Educational

Section 2
Into action: The practice of personal and social education: books for teachers

1 Young people in relationships
Coleman, J.C. (1980)
The Nature of Adolescence Methuen
A fresh look at young people in society and the basic issues which affect their lives.

Juniper, D. (1977)
>*Human Relationships in Schools and Colleges* Cresselles
>A very useful source book which looks at the practical issues
>of counselling and guidance in the curriculum.

Tuson, J. (1978)
>*Links: Personal Relationships* Stanley Thorne
>This book takes a general look at the relationships between
>the individual and the groups he finds himself in: family,
>friends and social groupings all receive attention.

2 Group work

Button, L. (1974)
>*Developmental Group Work with Adolescents* Hodder and
>Stoughton
>A basic source book for all teachers involved in group work
>with young people. The ideas voiced here are given active
>expression in *Group Tutoring for the Form Teacher* and
>*Active Tutorial Work*: see Section 3.1 of this Bibliography.

Button, L. (1976)
>*Developmental Group Work in the Secondary School:*
>*Pastoral Programme* Occasional Paper 1. Action Research
>Project, Department of Education, University of Swansea
>A brief but important paper on how group work may be
>incorporated into the pastoral work of a school in order to
>achieve its educational aims.

Douglas, T. (1983)
>*Groups: Understanding People Gathered Together* Tavistock
>A discussion of what constitutes a group and makes it
>function, and how we can develop insights into group
>dynamics.

Hamblin, D. (1983)
>*Guidance for the 16–19 Age Group* Basil Blackwell
>A very useful book containing activities and resources to
>develop survival skills for young adults.

Milson, F. (1973)
>*An Introduction to Group Work Skill* Routledge and Kegan
>Paul
>A very good book, written about adult action groups, which
>discusses the dynamics and effects of group work. Well
>worth reading.

Stanford, G. (1977)
>*Developing Effective Classroom Groups* Hart

Stech, E. and Ratcliffe, S.A. (1979)
Working in Groups National Textbook Company/Careers Consultants
Another excellent book which looks at the dynamics of interpersonal relationships. The book provides guidance in setting up group work and discusses the strategies involved and their effects.

Webb, C. (1978)
Communication Skills: an Approach to Personal Development Macmillan

3 Strategies for teachers: devising materials

Blythe, J., Brace, D. and Henry, T. (1978)
Teaching Social and Life Skills National Extension College in association with the Association for Liberal Education
A fine book, which deals with the issues and strategies appropriate to teaching social and life skills. It is geared to the 16+ range, but is applicable to secondary schools as well.

Brandes, D. and Phillips, H. (1979)
The Gamester's Handbook Hutchinson
A most useful book of games aimed at developing personal and social skills. A feature is that many games require minimal or no resources, and can be used at different levels of personal and social skills.

Davidson, A. and Gordon, P. (1978)
Games and Simulations in Action Woburn Press
Another useful book describing the theory as well as the practice of games for developing personal and social skills. The games here require planning, but are well worth the time.

Hopson, B. and Hough, P. (1979)
Exercises in Personal and Career Development 2nd edition CRAC (Hobsons Limited)
A very useful, practical book for helping students in their personal relationships and in their career development.

Hopson, B. and Scally, M. (1981)
Lifeskills Teaching McGraw-Hill
An excellent book, packed with practical hints on devising materials and using them. There is advice to the teacher on adopting an approach that will lead to his own and his students' personal development.

Manpower Services Commission
  Life Skills Training Manual Youth Employment Programme
  C.S.V. (NYP)
  This book identifies the skills of life and social skills, and
  provides some resource material for classroom use in
  teaching those skills.

Priestley, P., McGuire, J., Flegg, D., Hemsley, V. and Welham, D.
(1978)
  Social Skills and Personal Problem Solving Tavistock
  Publications
  This is a very useful book which gives practical guidance to
  teachers wanting to develop their own materials.

Stanton, G.P., Clark, E.P., Stradling, R. and Watts, A.G. (1980)
  Developing Social and Life Skills Further Education
  Curriculum Review and Development Unit
  An excellent book, aimed at the 16+ age-range, but
  appropriate for secondary education as well. It provides
  clear guidance to teachers with frameworks and criteria for
  the selection of content. Copies are free from the FEU.

4 Teaching children with individual needs

Best, R., Ribbons, P., Jarvis, C., and Oddy, D. (1983)
  Education and Care Heinemann Educational
  This book examines the implications for a pastoral scheme
  based on two years' research in a comprehensive school.

Harrop, A. (1983)
  Behaviour Modification in the Classroom Hodder and
  Stoughton
  A very useful book, full of practical hints on how to deal
  with reluctant and disruptive learners.

Lindsay, G. (ed) (1983)
  Problems of Adolescence in Secondary Schools Croom Helm
  A comprehensive guide to dealing with social problems in
  school, including coping with reluctant and hostile learners.

Olweus, D. (1978)
  Aggression in the Schools Halstead Press
  This study analyses why so many adolescent boys become
  involved in aggressive incidents.

Saunders, M. (1979)
  Class Control and Behaviour Problems McGraw-Hill
  A really excellent book aimed at helping teachers to develop
  their own techniques for overcoming problems of
  unacceptable behaviour in class.

Sluckin, A. (1981)
Growing up in the Playground: the Social Development of Children Routledge
The author suggests that perhaps the playground is as valuable a learning ground as the classroom as preparation for adult life.

Tattum, D.P. (1982)
Disruptive Pupils in Schools and Units John Wiley
This very useful book examines why pupils become disruptive, and examines the problems and practice of special units.

5 Health and sex education

Most of these resources are aimed at pupils' use (see section 3.2 of this Bibliography). Some useful books for teachers are:

Cowley, J., David, K., Williams, T.
Health Education in Schools Harper and Row

Dalzell-Ward, A.J.
A Textbook of Health Education Tavistock Educational

Schools Council, Health Education 5–13 Project (1977)
All About Me and *Think Well* Thomas Nelson and Sons

Schools Council. Home Economics in the Middle Years (8–13) Project (1979)
Home and Family Forbes

Schools Council. Health Education 13–18 Project (1980)
Co-ordinator's Guide Schools Council

Tanner, J.M. (1978)
Education and Physical Growth Hodder and Stoughton Educational

6 Counselling in schools

Hamblin, D. (1974)
The Teacher and Counselling Basil Blackwell
This is a very good book outlining the basic skills of counselling. It emphasises the point that the trained counsellor must be part of the total pastoral network of the school to act most effectively in the pupils' interests. It includes an extensive bibliography.

Jones, A. (1977)
Counselling Adolescents in School Kegan Press
A very useful source book, examining the needs of children in schools and why counselling should be necessary.

Munro, C. (1983)
> *Counselling: A Skills Approach* Tavistock
> A useful book, giving practical advice.

Noonan, E. (1983)
> *Counselling Young People* Methuen
> This book explores the complexities of counselling both in the theory and the practice.

Thompson, C.L. and Rudolph, L.B.
> *Counselling Children* Brooks Cole
> A comprehensive study of the theory and practice of counselling.

7 Careers guidance

Most of the books available are for pupils' use (see section 3.3. of this Bibliography). The short selection presented here is for teachers' use.

Avent, C. (1976)
> *Practical Approaches to Careers Education* CRAC (Hobsons Limited)
> A practical teacher's book of ideas and resources.

Hayes, J. and Hopson, B. (1972)
> *Careers Guidance: the Role of the School in Vocational Development.* Heinemann Educational
> A very useful book, containing some pupils' materials as well as ideas for the teacher.

Howden, R. and Dowson, H. (1973)
> *Practical Guidance in Schools* Careers Consultants
> Preparation for work may be included in the pastoral syllabus, and this book indicates how.

Jackson, R. (ed) (1973)
> *Careers Guidance: Practice and Problems* Edward Arnold
> A series of essays that investigate careers guidance in secondary schools

Section 3
Materials for personal and social education
Books for use in class

1 Tutorial work: formal schemes

Baldwin, J. and Wells, H. (1979–82)
> *Active Tutorial Work: Years 1 and 2; Years 3, 4 and 5; 6th Form* Basil Blackwell

A comprehensive scheme, covering the whole of secondary school life, which provides guidance and resources in tutorial work. Much in the books stems from the original ideas and papers of Leslie Button.

Button. L. (1981)
Group Tutoring for the Form Teacher Hodder and Stoughton
Leslie Button's own work, published as workbooks for years 1 and 2, and for years 3, 4 and 5. Again, there are many ideas and materials for class use.

Hopson, B. and Hough, P. (1979)
Exercises in Personal and Career Development CRAC (Hobsons Limited)
A series of teaching programmes and exercises based on the needs of young people, to develop their awareness of the world about them.

McGuire, J. and Priestley, P. (1981)
Life after School: a Social Skills Curriculum Pergamon Press
This book is intended for use with 16+ students but much is relevant to secondary education, particularly with a view to the transition from school to work.

Priestley, P. et al. (1978)
Social Skills and Personal Problem Solving Tavistock Publications
A series of teaching programmes and exercises. A very useful book.

2 Materials for health education
Most of these materials come in multi-media packs. Here are some of them:
Lifeline
McPhail, P., Chapman, H., and Ungoed-Thomas, J.R. Longmans, 1972
Already mentioned in this Bibliography, Section 1.2, the book resulting from the Schools Council Moral Education Project, *Moral Education in the Secondary School*. The kit also contains pupils' materials; *In Other People's Shoes, Sensitivity, Consequences, Points of View, Proving the Rule, What Would you Have Done?*

Schools Council Health Education 5–13
Thomas Nelson and Sons, 1977
This kit comprises two courses: *All About Me*, aimed for first and middle school use, and *Think Well* for middle school use. There are spirit masters and resource sheets, as well as teachers' guides.

Living Well: Health Education 12–18
> Health Education Council Project. Cambridge University Press, 1977.
> A set of workcards catering for the interests of young people in middle and secondary education. Contains the book *Support Group.*

Social Education Kits
> Scottish Community Education Centre, 1979
> The kits comprise a teacher's book, and pupils' materials covering aspects relevant to school and transition to work.

Health and Social Studies Cassettes
> E.J. Arnold
> These tapes present information and stimulus materials for pupil use on many major social problems including drug-taking, sexuality and social expectations.

Other useful kits are:

The Schools Council/Nuffield Humanities Curriculum Project Heinemann Educational, 1971

Good Health: A course for 9–13-year-olds Collins Educational

Social Education Kits Macmillan, 1976

Schools Council Integrated Studies Project Oxford University Press

Look after Yourself Health Education Council

Looking after Yourself Health Education Council

3 Materials for careers education

There are a number of multi-media resource packs available. They include:
The Schools Council Careers Education and Guidance Project: Work: Part 1 – Self-awareness and Decision-making; Work: Part 2 – The way work shapes life; Work: Part 3 – Skills for transition to work, further education and sixth form. Longman

Hopson, B. and Hough, P. (1985)
> *Exercises in Personal and Career Development* CRAC, 2nd edn

Childwell Project (1973)
> *Design for Living* E.J. Arnold
> A social studies course dealing with responsibilities of adulthood, understanding children, the world of work, living today, the world around us.

Other useful books include:
Avent, C. (1978)
Practical Approaches to Careers Education Hobsons Limited
A very useful guide in setting up a careers education
programme as part of the pastoral work of a school.

Hayes, J. and Hopson, B. (1972)
Careers Guidance Heinemann Education
This book indicates how careers education is part of the
overall pastoral work of a school, and gives specific advice
on developing a programme.

Howden, R. and Dowson, H. (1979)
The School Leaver's Handbook Careers Consultants
A very useful guide, giving practical hints and guidance in
choosing the right job.

Matthew, V. and Smith, M. (1984)
Decisions at 13/14+ New edn. Hobsons Limited
A pupil's guide to options and careers choice.

Two useful reference books on resources:
Summerson, E.J. (1979)
Careers Information and Careers Libraries Careers
Consultants

*Handbook of Free Careers Information in the United
Kingdom* Careers Consultants

There is a great deal of literature available. An excellent bibliography
appears in *Lifeskills Teaching* by B. Hopson and M. Scally, McGraw-
Hill, 1981. Many titles are also available from CRAC (Hobsons Limited)
Bateman Street, Cambridge CB2 1LZ.

4 Materials for making decisions

Esso Students' Business Game (1975) CRAC (Hobsons Limited)
Useful to teach sixth-formers how to run a business.

Juniper, D.F. (1976)
Decision-making for Schools and Colleges Pergamon Press
This is a practical scheme aimed at fifth and sixth year
students, and teaches them decision-making skills.

Lynch, M. (1977)
It's Your Choice Edward Arnold
A resource pack, suitable for 13–16-year-olds.

Watts, A.G. and Elsom, D. (1974)
>*Deciding* CRAC (Hobsons Limited)
>A series of exercises, and other resources, aimed at teaching
>decision-making skills.

5 Materials for learning how to study

Baker, E. (1975)
>*A Guide to Study* BACIE
>A useful guide.

Bamman, H.A. and Brammer, L.M. (1969)
>*How to Study Successfully* Pacific Books
>A comprehensive guide to developing self-study, including
>how to improve academic skills, how to use resources, and
>how to concentrate.

Buzan, T. (1976)
>*Use Your Head* BBC Publications
>Based on the BBC programmes, this book is aimed primarily
>at adult learners, though the strategies described are
>appropriate to secondary education.

Carman, R.A. and Adams, W.R. (1972)
>*Study Skills: a Student's Guide for Survival* John Wiley
>All you want to know for sixth formers.

Open University
>*Preparing to Study* Open University
>This book is aimed at mature students, but is also a very
>useful guide for teachers in schools.

Parsons, C. (1976)
>*How to Study Effectively* Arrow
>A useful guide.

Rowntree, D. (1976)
>*Learn How to Study* Macdonald and Jane's
>Aimed at fifth and sixth year and college students.

6 Materials for role play

Basic Skills Unit (1981)
>*Using Role Play: an introductory guide.* Manpower Services
>Commission. Published by the National Extension College.
>An excellent introductory guide, full of practical hints and
>easy to use. Read it in an hour, and use its ideas indefinitely.

Brandes D. and H. Phillips (1979)
>*The Gamester's Handbook.* Hutchinson. (This is mentioned
>in the main Bibliography.) Many games here for group leaders
>to select.

Davison A. and P. Gordon. (1983)
Games and Simulations in Action. Woburn Press.
Many games and extended activities, invaluable for group leaders.

Moreno, J. (1964)
Psycho-drama. New York: Beacon House

Scher A. and C. Verral (1975)
100+ Ideas for Drama. Heinemann Educational.

Section 4
Implications for teachers

1 Evaluation

One of the issues tackled in this book is the need for an evaluation of the curriculum of personal and social education, of teaching methods, of in-service education. Evaluation is in a moving state at present, and a number of developing models are emerging rapidly. The following books are all excellent surveys of some crucial aspects.

Hamilton, D. et al. (eds) (1977)
Beyond the Numbers Game Macmillan Education
This excellent book traces the historical development of evaluation theory and practice, and points the way to future trends.

Henderson, E.S. (1978)
The Evaluation of In-Service Teacher Training Croom Helm
This is a valuable book that looks at the theory and practice of in-service teacher training and points to future developments

House, E.R. (1980)
Evaluating with Validity Sage Publications
This book examines the principles of evaluation, and struggles with the problem of how to keep evaluation fair.

Shipman, M. (1979)
In-School Evaluation Heinemann
A practical book, covering the evaluation of many aspects of school life, emphasising the crucial role that evaluation plays, and suggesting ways in which it might be most economically used.

Tawney, D. (ed) (1976)
Curriculum Evaluation Today: Trends and Implications
Schools Council Research Studies
An excellent collection of papers, looking at developments in techniques of evaluation and trends for the future.

2 Pupil Profiling

Balogh, J. (1982)
Profile Reports for School Leavers Schools Council/Longman
A review of early methods by schools to record the experiences, qualities and achievements of school-leavers at 16+, and a consideration of some of the implications for teachers, pupils, employers and administrators.

Burgess T. and Adams, E. (1980)
Outcomes of Education Macmillan
This book examines many alternatives to public examinations.

Department of Education and Science (1983)
Records of Achievement at 16: Some Examples of Current Practice HMSO
An account of the visits by a small team of HM inspectors to ten schools in England where records of achievement were in use. The paper raises issues concerning future development of such schemes.

Further Education Unit (1982)
Profiles: a Review of Issues and Practice in the Use and Development of Student Profiles
A collection of papers mainly about the state of the art of profiling in the FE sector.

Further Education Unit (1984)
Profiles and Graded Tests: the Technical Issues
As the title suggests; a very useful book.

Garforth, D. (1983)
Profile Assessment: Recording Student Progress. a School-Focused Inset Workshop Manual. Dorset County Council
The manual leads a school through the design and implementation of a scheme of Profile Assessment and relates the profile to the curriculum assessment, recording and reporting policies. Available from West Dorset Teachers' Centre, King Street, Bridport.

Goacher, B. (1983)
Recording Achievement at 16+ Schools Council/Longman
A review of the attempts of 21 schools to develop better documents for school-leavers, and the implications of their investigations at school, local and national level.

Schools Council for Wales
Profile Reporting in Wales
A discussion paper which followed a two-year feasibility study of introducing a nationally available pupil profile in Wales.

3 Inquiry in action

The literature of Action Research is growing, and the following books are key landmarks in this rapidly expanding field.

Carr, W. and Kemmis, S. (1982)
Becoming Critical: Knowing through Action Research
Deakin University Press
A recent development in the ideas of conducting educational research.

Corey, S. (1953)
Action Research to Improve School Practices Teachers College, Columbia University, New York

Elliot, J. (1953)
Paradigms of Educational Research and Theories of Schooling
Cambridge Action Research Network
John Elliott is a leading figure in the Action Research movement in Britain and has written extensively on the subject. This is one of his very useful publications.

Kemmis, S. and McTaggart, R.
The Action Research Planner Deakin University Press
A practical translation of the theory of Action Research into everyday use. An excellent guide.

Lewin, K. (1946)
'Action Research and Minority Problems' *Journal of Social Issues* Vol 2
This was the paper that first posed formally the idea of research in action.

McNiff, J. (1984)
'Action Research: a Generative Model for In-Service Support'
British Journal of In-Service Education Summer, 1984
A further development of the idea of Action Research and how it may be applied in in-service education

Nixon, J. (1981)
A Teacher's Guide to Action Research – Evaluation, Enquiry and Development in the Classroom Grant McIntyre
A collection of essays showing that the teacher is researcher, and that perhaps the most useful educational research is that day-to-day enquiry into what goes on in the ordinary classroom.

Reason, P. and Rowan, J. (eds) (1981)
Human Inquiry John Wiley
A collection of excellent papers covering the philosophy and practice of Action Research.

Stenhouse, L. (1975)

> *Introduction to Curriculum Research and Development*
> Heinemann
> An excellent book, discussing the whole question of what
> research is and its practical situation in class practice.

Whitehead, A.J. (1983)

> 'The Use of Personal Educational Theories' *British Journal of
> In-Service Education* Summer 1983
> Jack Whitehead spearheads the Action Research movement
> from the University of Bath School of Education. This paper
> is one of many that he has written.